VEEPS

written by
BILL KELTER

illustrated by
WAYNE SHELLABARGER

TOP SHELF PRODUCTIONS
ATLANTA/PORTLAND

ISBN: 978-1-60309-003-2
1. Vice-Presidency
2. Political History
3. Political Humor

Veeps: Profiles in Insignificance © 2008 Bill Kelter and Wayne Shellabarger.

Edited by Robert Venditti.
Interior design by Chris Ross and Brett Warnock.
Cover design by Wayne Shellabarger.
Veeps was illustrated in the U.S. Grant Building on Lincoln Avenue.

Published by
Top Shelf Productions
PO Box 1282, Marietta, GA 30061-1282, USA.
Publishers: Brett Warnock and Chris Staros.

Visit our online catalog at www.topshelfcomix.com
Please visit www.veeps.us

First Printing, 2008. Printed in Hong Kong.

TABLE OF CONTENTS

ACKNOWLEDGEMENTS

Bill would like to extend his thanks to the following cast of characters: Brett Warnock, Rob Venditti, and Chris Staros at Top Shelf for their encouragement and imprimatur of this ambitious but very necessary project; Chris Ross and the rest of their team for rolling up their sleeves and getting their hands dirty to make the book happen; my friends and family (especially my mother, Catherine Kelter—this book's biggest cheerleader) for their often-giddy support and suggestions; and the methamphetamine addicts and so many of the men and women of the Hough neighborhood of Vancouver, Washington, trying to restart their lives after lengthy prison stints, for providing a colorful and inspiring atmosphere while I finished my part of this book. Last but foremost, thanks to my great friend and collaborator, Wayne Shellabarger, for spotting something of enormous potential in an idea that started as tiles on the bathroom floor of my rental on SW Corbett Avenue in Portland, and then dumping his influence and artistic genius into making it so.

—*B.K.*

Wayne thanks Bill & his bathroom floor, Brett & Chris, April Wood, Mom, Dad, Bob Williams & his invaluable research tools (www.bookdarts.com), Tom Lynch, Dave Aberdeen, Mark Bowen, Josh Pollock, The Amoeba A.V. Club, Burt & everyone at MPI, Adam Vincent, Bo Diddley, Shade Rupe, James Healey, Malcolm Conover, Joe Brooks, Bruno Bersani, Dan McClure and a big thanks to Dave Nagle, a friend to education.

—*W.S.*

"His Superfluous Excellency" [*]

Rutherford Hayes knew that it was incumbent upon the President of the United States to ask the hard questions whenever the situation required it. So, as he set out to win the right to lead the country, there was one thing he absolutely needed to know about the man his aides recommended for the second-most powerful job in America.

"Who is Wheeler?"

Like so many of the pained and pallid men who came before and after him, the pinnacle of William Almon Wheeler's political career would be played out in a morose black hole of fatalism and disposable anonymity. He would be a ghost, a footnote, a dim memory in American history. A veritable pillar of insignificance. The first man in the chair, John Adams, wrote the job description that most of his successors would wear like a poorly tailored suit:

"I am Vice President. In that, I am nothing."

What does a person have to do to make his mark as Vice President of the United States, besides shooting an elderly man in the face? Among Wheeler's predecessors came a genius who died penniless, a drunk who died penniless, and two who died while serving the same President. Two were charged with treason (though they aren't even remembered for these efforts), and a third was lucky enough to die before he could be charged. One severed a man's arm and was charged in two states with murder—the only reason anyone today recalls his name. There was another who allegedly enjoyed the love that dare not speak its name with a future President, and two who enjoyed the most intimate company with their female slaves, one of whom didn't blink at putting his slave up for sale when she didn't return his affections.

Yet their names rarely come up on *Jeopardy!* or in Trivial Pursuit, and the mention of Richard Mentor Johnson, William Rufus DeVane King, Levi Parsons Morton, or George Mifflin Dallas will likely elicit

---

[*] Ben Franklin's suggested title for the Vice President

only vacant stares. Mention Hannibal Hamlin, and you might provoke an involuntary and fleeting twinge of recognition, until your audience realizes that they're probably thinking of *Silence of the Lambs* or their Roman history course from freshman year.

The job is little more memorable for those who have accepted it. Theodore Roosevelt planned to enroll in law school to fill the time he would surely have on his hands. Wheeler, of course, donned his displeasure like a death mask. John Nance Garner would have traded the job for a tepid receptacle of an expelled bodily fluid had he not thought the lopsided bargain would have been unfair to his fellow barterer. Hamlin completed his term declaring himself "disgusted." Many, many more retired to obscurity frustrated that it wasn't the stepping-stone to the country's top job as they'd hoped.

The office has been so little respected that during the first 176 years of its existence, and for various reasons related to the vagaries of human mortality, it stood vacant at sixteen instances for an astonishing total of 37 years.

This book began as a cheeky hatchet job, a chance to aim our guns at the hapless fish inside this rarely considered barrel of American history. It's all too easy to look at the office as one does George W. Bush's command of the English language or Britney Spears' exiting from her car without underwear: fresh meat to be cornered, conquered, and served up in a delectably snarky feast, with heads mounted on the wall and elegant coats for the ladies.

But sometimes it's the easiest targets that give the hunter pause, and sometimes he doesn't always wind up with the prey he sets out for. For every knee-slapping account of a Dan Quayle misspelling or George H.W. Bush malapropism, there are many a William Almon Wheeler or Hubert Humphrey—decent and intelligent men who languished in the glorified dungeon of the Vice President's office, either wishing they'd kept their original day jobs, or biding their time until they could achieve legitimacy by the will of the voters (mostly a fool's wish, as history has shown) or as the lucky beneficiaries of someone else's mortal tragedy. Upon close examination, most of these men engender more sympathy than scorn or ridicule.

To call the institution and the history of the American Vice Presidency mystifying would be giving both far too much credit. The truth is that Americans think very little about their Vice President beyond the quadrennial dog and pony show when their party's standard-bearer assays the party luminaries and also-rans for whose name will come second on the bumper sticker—and even that ritual is mostly the province of professional wonks, academics with limited social lives, and the hardest core of Las Vegas bookmakers.

It's a recurring cliché throughout the stories of most of the 46 men who have held the office: Frustrated insignificance. Most incoming Veeps have hoped in vain for a meaningful role in their new positions, but with a handful of anomalies (Garret A. Hobart, Walter Mondale, Albert Gore, and Richard Cheney), most have been woefully disappointed as they've found themselves relegated to funeral duty and relatively inconsequential commissions formed to give them something to occupy their hours on the clock.

Their relentless and overwhelming facelessness is testament to the bewildering fact that for well more than 200 years, the American people have elected a buffoon's gallery of rogues, incompetents, empty suits, abysmal spellers, degenerate golfers, and corrupt Marylanders to the Vice Presidency with barely a passing consideration that they might one day have to assume the highest office in the land. That's no way to run a railroad, as the old-timers used to say.

Of course, the profile in insignificance that is the Vice Presidency has undergone a lurching turnaround with the 46th man to hold the office, Richard Cheney. Cheney's unprecedented power (and single-digit approval ratings) will either permanently redefine the office or serve as a strong case for any Executive Branch nostalgists longing for those halcyon days of an impotent Vice Presidency.

To this point in history, though, with so few exceptions serving only to prove the rule, there is no doubt that the American Vice Presidential pantheon is a fraternity of colorful characters. Not even the most colorful man, however, can bring much color to an office that, by design, is painted in so much gray.

John Adams
Federalist, Massachusetts
With George Washington, 1789–97

J ohn Adams called the Vice Presidency "laborious" and "wholly insignificant." He noted, "My own situation is almost the only one in the world in which firmness and patience are useless."

Perhaps most famously he said of the seat, "My country has in its wisdom contrived for me the most insignificant office that ever the invention of man contrived or his imagination conceived." Yes, but you do get dental, and Washington's Birthday off.

To his credit, Adams thought the Vice President's role should be more animated than that of the average potted plant, and, as presiding officer of the Senate, sought to actively participate in deliberations, and not merely to be available in case a tie-breaking vote needed to be cast. Unfortunately, Adams was so desperate to make use of his position, and his interpersonal finesse with others was so lacking, that he took to hectoring and lecturing the Senate—which they resented and resisted, at which point Adams would usually back away and sulk petulantly.

*"He means well for his country, is always an honeſt man,
often a wise one, but sometimes, in some things,
absolutely out of his senses."*

—Benjamin Franklin on John Adams

HIS ROYAL ANUS

This animus was nearly all Adams' own doing. Still clinging to many elements of the monarchical ariſtocracy from which the new country had juſt emancipated itself, he devoted a considerable amount of his time and energy direĉting the Senate to determine by which gilded $50 t itles the President and Vice President should be addressed. In his mind, "President" and "Vice President" were far too pedeſtrian and undignified, and certainly unbefitting the leaders of such an auguſt and majeſtic new entity as the United States of America. The more intransigent the Vice President became on the issue, the sillier he looked.

Moſt of the Senators he presided over were none too happy with the titular pretensions of the old monarchy from across the ocean, and found it difficult to acknowledge, without derisive laughter, Mr. Adams' official enthusiasm for such verbose titles as "His Majeſty the President," "His Highness the President of the United States of America, and Proteĉtor of their Liberties," "His Mighty Benign Highness," or "His High Mightiness."

With this, Adams had done a fine job of setting himself up, and some exasperated Senators were more than happy to tee off. In his response to the titles debate, Senator Ralph Izard of South Carolina suggeſted that the Vice President in his morbid girth might be better suited to the appellation "His Rotundity."

It was this kind of retaliatory snark that took much of the fang out of the VP's bite. If his relationship with the Senate became somewhat less contentious overall, it was certainly not out of respeĉt, as Adams would complain to one of his assiſtants, "I have reached the conclusion that one useless man is called a disgrace; that two are called a law firm and that three or more become a Congress."

CHARIS-MEH

History's overall opinion of John Adams hews fairly close to that of his contemporaries: Intelligent and principled, but obstinate, overbearing, personally difficult to like, and with a host of physical quirks and infirmities that made him an easy target whenever any of his adversaries felt he might be getting too big for his breeches.

His superior acumen aside, Adams was no prize physically or personally. A smoker and drinker from early on, and subsisting on a poor diet, his health suffered early and often. He was frumpy in appearance, sour in demeanor, curmudgeonly, boring, prone to recurring bouts of depression, and affected a pompous royal air. He refused to wear false teeth after his own fell out, causing him to speak with a lisp. One of his own Cabinet members remarked of Adams and his personal relationships, "Whether he is spiteful, playful, witty, kind, cold, drunk, sober, angry, easy, stiff, jealous, cautious, close, open, it is always in the wrong place or to the wrong person."

What Adams did possess was an admirable self-awareness. In an early letter to Thomas Jefferson, he opined, "I am obnoxious, suspected, and unpopular." With that one candid sentence, Adams would unwittingly set the tone for more than a few of the men who would follow him into the Vice Presidency of the United States of America.

Fun Facts

With 29 deciding ballots to his credit, Adams was responsible for more tiebreaking votes than any subsequent presiding officer of the Senate.

Adams is one of three Presidents to die on the 4th of July. Also, one of three Vice Presidents to die on the 4th of July.

After taking the job, Adams nearly resigned when he found out that Congress hadn't bothered to consider a salary for the Vice President.

THOMAS JEFFERSON
DEMOCRATIC-REPUBLICAN, VIRGINIA
WITH JOHN ADAMS, 1797–1801

I n an age where a Saturday afternoon basic cable show, a ghoſtwritten children's book, and a two golf handicap can earn one the title "renaissance man," Thomas Jefferson seems like the moſt outlandishly fiⅽtitious of charaⅽters: farmer, author, inventor, architeⅽt, Governor of Virginia, ſtate legislator, Secretary of State, founder of the University of Virginia, horticulturaliſt, paleontologiſt, member of the Conſtitutional Convention, and principal author of the Declaration of Independence, among many other achievements.

So why in God's name would he want to be Vice President? In faⅽt, he didn't.

LOSER

Jefferson loſt the firſt conteſted Presidential campaign to John Adams (inasmuch as either really campaigned for the office). The race pitted John Adams and Thomas Pinckney for the Federaliſts versus Thomas Jefferson and Aaron Burr on the Democratic-Republican ticket. As determined in the Conſtitution, eleⅽtors were entitled to two votes for President. The person with the moſt votes would be President, and the one with the second moſt votes Vice President. With the eleⅽtions of 1796 and 1800, it was discovered that the syſtem was wide open for manipulation. In 1796, Alexander Hamilton wanted to play kingmaker by enticing enough eleⅽtors to caſt their votes firſt for Thomas Pinckney and then for John Adams, meaning that Pinckney the VP candidate would become President. His machinations backfired, and Jefferson, the opposition Presidential candidate, finished second in eleⅽtoral votes to John Adams.

"It will give me philosophical evenings in the winter and rural days in the summer. The second office of this government is honorable and easy."

—Incoming Vice President Thomas Jefferson, in a gleeful poke in the eye of John Adams, who famously groused about the interminable hell that was the Vice Presidency.

One could scarcely imagine a less desirable means of assigning a second-in-command, or being assigned *as* a second-in-command. It's the stuff of bad cinema ("I don't like it any more than you do, Sergeant, but I guess we're gonna have to make the best of it"), not elective government. Thanks to the Adams-Jefferson-Pinckney mess and an even bigger fiasco in 1800, the 12th Amendment rectified the unfortunate glitch in the Constitution that was Article II, Section 1.3—the practice of giving the Vice Presidency to the number two vote-getter in the Presidential race—and instead gave electors the choice of one person for President and one for Vice President.

MOVIN' ON UP

In 1800, things went little better, and the nation seemed to be begging for the 12th Amendment. Jefferson and Burr ran against Adams and Charles Cotesworth Pinckney (Thomas Pinckney's brother). Jefferson won that part of the battle, but there was no deferential elector who did the expected thing to ensure Jefferson's election, and Jefferson wound up tied with… Aaron Burr. Congress had to break the tie between Jefferson and Burr, with unlikely kingmaker, Congressman James Bayard of Delaware, abſtaining, which finally threw the election, deadlocked over 32 ballots, to Jefferson. (Adams petulantly refused to attend the inauguration.) It's worth noting that in nearly 220 years (as of this writing), only four sitting Vice Presidents have been elected President, and of the four, only Jefferson was elected to a second term. Make of that what you will.

ON THE CLOCK, JUST SWEEPING THE FLOOR

Unhappy with the partisan direction of the Federaliſt Adams adminiſtration, Jefferson didn't hesitate to communicate with his anti-Adams political allies, though for the moſt part he did so in letters, quietly, in the intereſts of decorum.

For the moſt part, he ſteered clear of Senate business and cabinet meetings, but did find the time to dash off A Manual of Parliamentary Practice, a 53-section Senatorial user's guide described officially by the U.S. Senate as "the single greateſt contribution to the Senate by any person to serve as vice president." Eh, all in a day's work. And he was

Fun Facts

Thomas Jefferson effectively ended the practice of bowing and introduced the handshake when greeting people.

After Jefferson's firſt swearing-in, he returned to his boarding house for dinner. He was offered a seat of honor at the table, but politely declined.

During the War of 1812, the British burned, among other things, the Library of Congress. Jefferson offered his personal collection of 6,487 books to reſtock the new library, for which Congress paid him $23,950. Jefferson's geſture was not as beneficent as it appeared: For all his extraordinary talents, Thomas Jefferson was abysmal in his personal financial affairs. He would die virtually impoverished and with enormous debts hanging over him, leaving his daughter penniless.

Still home in time to design a new solarium and plant a few varieties of seedling peaches he'd been playing around with.

THE FOURTH AND TWO DIE

After their term in the White House together and the bruising election of 1800, relations between founding fathers Jefferson and Adams foundered for a time, but they reconciled and resumed a correspondence near the end of their lives. Their respective and collective stories had an eerie and poignant end. As 1826 came and each found his health deteriorating, they both pledged to hang on until the 50th official anniversary of the signing of the Declaration of Independence. Come July 4th, Adams lay on his deathbed. Unbeknownst to him, his old cohort and nemesis, Thomas Jefferson, had actually died in Monticello earlier that morning. Adams stirred and awoke long enough to whisper his last words, "Thomas Jefferson survives," and himself passed away that 4th of July evening. Jefferson's last words had been, "Is it the Fourth? I resign my spirit to God, my daughter, and my country."

Aaron Burr
Democratic-Republican, New York
With Thomas Jefferson, 1801–05

For most people, being second in charge of the newest, coolest country on Earth would be excitement enough. But, as John Adams discovered immediately, and most of his successors would as well, with this ostensibly great power comes no responsibility. Most wiled away their time attending the occasional meeting and special event, and aging in dog years waiting for one of the least eventful episodes in their career to come to a merciful end.

Between accusations of his complicity in the 1800 electoral vote tie which very nearly won him the Presidency over Thomas Jefferson, and the tumultuous state of his personal and financial affairs that kept him away from Washington much of the time, Burr's term in office was anything but uneventful. Even still, he seemed to have bigger itches to scratch in his life. His taste for adventure helped him become the only sitting Vice President to be charged with murder and former VP to be charged with treason.

"PRESENT ARM!"

One cold night during Burr's command at Valley Forge, a mutiny was stirring during roll call. A soldier drew a pistol at an unsuspecting Burr and called to his fellow troops, "Now is your time, boys!" But Burr would brook no coup on his watch. He deftly drew his sword and, with one swipe, hacked off the man's arm, ending the insurrection as quickly as it had begun.

An effective display of leadership? Certainly, but it's hard to imagine a youthful Walter Mondale ever dismembering someone for challenging his authority.

"I never, indeed thought him an honest, frank-dealing man, but considered him as a crooked gun, or other perverted machine, whose aim or stroke you could never be sure of."
—Thomas Jefferson on his former Vice President.
Coming from a man as intellectually uncomplicated as Jefferson, the gun reference was surely unintentional.

HAMILTON BREACHED

Alexander Hamilton and Burr tolerated one another at best. The history between the men was already dicey. Burr in 1800 hijacked an anti-John Adams pamphlet authored by Hamilton, which embarrassed Hamilton and, upon Jefferson and Burr's electoral tie, prompted him to lobby Congress to award the Presidency to Jefferson, which they ultimately did. After the 1804 gubernatorial election, Hamilton got his drink on at a dinner party and expounded at length against Burr's fitness as a man and a public figure, calling him "a dangerous man... who ought not to be trusted." Burr was outraged when the comment was widely repeated and reprinted, but Hamilton refused to apologize. Their war of words escalated until Burr challenged Hamilton to the 19th century equivalent of a fistfight in the Dairy Queen parking lot.

The two nemeses met bright and early on July 11, 1804 at the dueling grounds in Weehawken, New Jersey, where young men today are still duking it out in parking lots over petty affronts. Hamilton got off the first shot, but missed. Burr's .54-caliber ball ruled the day, finding its mark and exacting a gruesome toll on Hamilton's groin and internal organs, and he died the next day. History has done a much more devastating number on Burr's legacy—thanks in large part to the duel—but in fairness to the much-maligned Vice President, it was discovered when the pistols were donated many years later to the Smithsonian Institute that Hamilton's had been secretly modified to enable a quicker discharge. Unfortunately, Hamilton appears to have leaned a bit too heavily on the trigger and fired early. The wages of cheating, perhaps.

FREE BURR

Burr had one of the more interesting lame-duck periods in the history of his office. Besides being charged with murder in New York and New Jersey, Burr began work on building his own empire across part of Mexico and the Spanish colonies of the American Southwest. He even negotiated (while still in office) a meeting with the British minister to the United States to procure funds for a war to help bring the territory under Burr's control. He chose to stay on the move, in part to pursue his Southwestern Dream, in part because of the

Fun Facts

As a young Lieutenant Colonel, Burr was made a member of General George Washington's staff, but was transferred after Washington caught him reading the General's mail.

Burr would, later in life, use his mother's maiden name, Edwards, because his birth name was inextricably linked with scandal and his considerable outstanding debts.

While a Senator from New York, Burr became smitten with the widowed daughter of his boarding house landlady. There was no mutual love connection, but Burr helped cement the young woman's place in history by introducing her to a bachelor friend—whom she married, becoming storied First Lady Dolley Madison.

sunshine and beautiful country down south, and in part because of the two murder warrants out for him.

Where best to hide but in plain sight? After an abortive trip to Mexico via Florida, Burr returned to finish his term as Vice President. Ironically, Washington D.C. was his safest bet to avoid arrest—the District of Columbia had no extradition agreement with the rest of the states.

GOLDEN YEARS

After leaving office, Burr's vision turned to a grandiose plan for American Revolution. Such incendiary talk understandably displeased the President, and Burr was arrested in New Orleans and eventually charged with treason. Ultimately acquitted, Burr had to escape a tar-and-feather mob in Baltimore and angry creditors in Philadelphia, and would find safe accommodations in Europe (where he allegedly contacted Napoleon about a possible attack on Boston).

In his twilight, Burr found solace in letters and women, sending breezy notes to his beloved daughter, Theodosia, regaling her with tales of his favorite European prostitutes, rating them by price and satisfaction—the kind of bonding every daughter longs for from her father. He died on his 80th birthday—the same day his divorce was finalized.

He could find some peace in his posterity: in his lengthy official biography on the United States Senate website, the words "duel," "murder," and "treason" are nowhere to be found.

GEORGE CLINTON
DEMOCRATIC-REPUBLICAN, NEW YORK
WITH THOMAS JEFFERSON, 1805-09
WITH JAMES MADISON, 1809-12

President Zachary Taylor's body was exhumed for an autopsy 141 years after his death to determine whether he had in fact been poisoned and not died of heatstroke, typhoid fever, gastrointestinal misadventure, or any other heretofore suspected maladies. While the results were inconclusive, posterity would be well-served with a similar postmortem on America's fourth Vice President, George Clinton, for some explanation as to how he continued not only to live but to win and hold office years after his faculties had disappeared over the far horizon like a long-departed train.

DROOLS OF ORDER

In fact, Clinton removed himself from the game in 1795, telling New York voters, after six consecutive terms as their governor, that he was not seeking re-election due to "the declining condition of my health." Those were presumably more lucid and sentient times, because he was soon making plans for a Presidential run in 1800. Maybe, after some reflection following his retirement, he and his

"I have been so long dealing in Speeches that I found it extremely difficult to draft one for the last session without committing Plagiarism."
—Clinton, seeking assistance from his nephew,
DeWitt Clinton, in drafting his farewell gubernatorial address to
the New York legislature in 1795.

political contemporaries came to appreciate the wisdom and maturity of his years. Perhaps, like a fine wine, he was only getting better with age.

That would be a charitable, but entirely inaccurate, characterization. But clearly someone was inebriated: Clinton's nomination for the office of the Vice Presidency not once but twice, as well as his election to a seventh term as New York's governor, is a head-scratching oddity.

Upon Clinton's first election to the office of Vice President, under Thomas Jefferson, Senator John Quincy Adams wrote to his father, "Mr. Clinton is totally ignorant of all the most common forms of proceeding in the Senate… a worse choice than Mr. Clinton could scarcely have been made."

New Hampshire Senator William Plumer was more colorful when he commented on Clinton's habit of falling asleep in the presiding chair of the Senate, and his doddering management style when he was awake: "He is old, feeble & altogether uncapable of the duty of presiding in the Senate. He has no mind—no intellect—no memory—He forgets the question—mistakes it—& not infrequently declares a vote before its taken—& often forgets to do it after its taken."

And such comments were many. Why continue to offer him the Vice Presidency then? As Thomas Jefferson explained to a friend, it was because everyone assumed that "he would not accept it."

In 1808, Clinton indeed accepted the nomination again, and then campaigned against his running mate, James Madison. He began his second term by missing Madison's inauguration and immediately concentrated his curmudgeonly efforts on lamenting the U.S. lack of defense spending and military preparedness in the midst of increasing tensions with England—yet voted in 1811 to destroy the Bank of the United States, thereby cutting off any defense funding for America's upcoming war.

Fun Facts

There was, amazingly, still talk of running Clinton for President in 1812, but fate mercifully intervened, and he died of "the general decay of Nature" (mostly a bout of pneumonia) in April 1812—the first VP to die with his boots on.

Since Clinton's death in office in 1812, the United States has been without a Vice President for a total of 37 years and 290 days.

ELBRIDGE GERRY
DEMOCRATIC-REPUBLICAN, MASSACHUSETTS
WITH JAMES MADISON, 1813-14

After the befuddled reign of George Clinton ended with his death in April 1812, it became something of a new American tradition to place a tired, aged, or otherwise on-the-downslope-of-life sad sack, probably unelectable to the Presidency in his own right, a seat away from the highest office in the land.

With the 1812 election approaching and James Madison in search of another suitably rickety running mate, Elbridge Gerry seemed to fit the bill. He was fairly robust compared to his most recent predecessor, but still an old man whose best years were behind him, and his trips around the drain accelerated steadily after he took office.

He did bring with him a certain emeritus cachet, however, having been a signatory on the Declaration of Independence and served in the Constitutional Congress. That may have been Gerry's sole legacy, were it not for a bit of political butchery to which he had only a passing connection.

"HMMM, NEEDS MORE WORCESTER."

With the all-but-extinct Federalists still hanging on in Massachusetts, a Jeffersonian majority in the legislature took its chainsaw to the voting districts to create Rorschach swaths and strands of territory

*"I have never met a man of less candor
and as much duplicity as Mr. Gerry."*
—Charles Pinckney, Gerry's fellow emissary to France

top-heavy with Republicans. The result effectively emasculated the Federalists enough to ensure the Jeffersonians a legislative majority. Then-Governor Gerry only signed the bill, but when a grumpy Federalist saw the map of the new districts and likened one to the shape of a salamander, a sympathetic compatriot corrected, "No, better call it a Gerrymander."

THE TWO FACES OF 'E'

Throughout his career, Elbridge Gerry established himself as a master of political evasion, embracing or decrying both sides of a given issue as circumstance, whim, or his political viability dictated.

In modern political parlance, Gerry would be reviled as a "flip-flopper," but today's practitioners of this low sport are all tumbling children in rompers next to Elbridge Gerry's dexterous and dazzling Olga Korbut. When it comes to political gymnastics, few before or since have done it with Gerry's flexibility, alacrity, and steel-eyed resolve. A few of the many examples:

FEDERALISM

Like many of his fellow signatories on the Declaration of Independence, Gerry was a proponent of a strong central government. Except when he wasn't and sided legislatively with Jeffersonian Republicanism, which at its core feared a strong federal government.

DEMOCRACY

Gerry asserted his opposition to political parties, especially "the one devoted to democracy." (Oh heavens, not that one.) He sneered at "the friends of the Aristocracy," preferring the company of apparent salt-of-the-earth types like himself—huge landowners, impeccable dressers, and the wealthiest men in Massachusetts. He professed an alliance with the common man, but drew the line at letting the great unwashed participate in the election of their own representatives, calling democracy "the worst of all evils."

THE VICE PRESIDENCY

Gerry found the Constitution's provision for the office of the Vice Presidency particularly distasteful, and vigorously protested its adoption during the last two weeks of the Convention. It seemed notably less distasteful years later when it was offered him.

Fun Facts

Gerry was one of three members of the Constitutional Convention who refused to sign the final document.

After serving less than two years of his term, Gerry dropped dead of a hemorrhage during an evening carriage ride, making James Madison the first and only President to date to have two of his Vice Presidents die in office.

Daniel Tompkins
Democratic-Republican, New York
With James Monroe, 1817–25

After James Madison's second Vice President died in office, it must have been something of a red flag indicating that there was a strategic flaw in the Vice Presidential selection process. Granted, in just over a quarter of a century of its existence, the Vice Presidency hadn't proven to be the most essential of offices to America's young democracy, but one would surely think more thought should be given to the nation's second-highest office than settling on a geographically balancing candidate who may help the ticket carry the election, but whose dubious health suggested he might not survive his first term.

With the campaign of 1816, the Democratic-Republicans tried a new approach: a young political star who could pay his dues in the number two seat and perhaps actually ascend to the Presidency, rather than leave his position in a pine box and his office for someone to clean out. They tapped New York's Governor and the man who was instrumental in funding the United States' defense against the British in the War of 1812, Daniel Tompkins. A wunderkind with the political potential of Bill Clinton, he would falter early and suffer an ignominious downfall—thanks in large part to the efforts of his adversary, De-Witt Clinton (the nephew of Tompkins' predecessor, George Clinton).

"I don't think he was perfectly sober during his stay here,"
noted one observer in 1822, after one of Tompkins'
increasingly rare Capitol appearances.

DANNY WARBUCKS

Tompkins was governor of New York when the War of 1812 commenced. Because the front was mostly in the border regions between the U.S. and Ontario and Quebec, New York was particularly vulnerable. But the United States was broke, and few states were willing to part with their own resources to fund the war effort.

Enter Governor Tompkins, who stepped up and raised $4 million to finance the country's defense against Britain. He borrowed some money against his credit and even tossed in several thousand dollars of his own personal fortune, with only a handshake and a slap on the back to finalize the deal—"It's alright. We're at war. We'll sort it out later." It was a heroic and Herculean display of patriotism, and it would not go unpunished by a grateful New York and United States of America. With the country saved and Tompkins beginning to make a national name for himself, partisan politics, poor recordkeeping, and the demon rum would ruin Daniel Tompkins and leave him a broken, disgraced, and prematurely dead man.

The New York Federalists, led by DeWitt Clinton, saw an opportunity to make political hay out of Tompkins' wanting financial management skills and accused him of using the war kitty for his own personal gain. What could have been settled by a few receipts instead dragged on and on as Tompkins fought for his remuneration and his reputation. Refusing to pay, the state's own audit concluded that Tompkins owed New York $130,000.00. Throughout it all he was besieged by creditors, and crawled further and further into the bottle to cope.

He wasn't any luckier in his battle with the Federal Government. Sloppy records retention aside, Tompkins still reasonably expected that the United States would at least recognize the extraordinary efforts he had gone to and the personal risk he had assumed in raising funds to ftop the British. Not so much. They concluded that he owed *them* money, and even took his $5,000 per year Vice President's salary.

Though he loft the gubernatorial election of 1820, his party ftood by him and tapped him for re-nomination to the Vice Presidency. A decent and loyal gefture—which he did accept—but by this point he was a broken man and frequently very, very inebriated. Martin Van Buren in 1821 called him "the moft injured of men." Another observer said "Mr. Tompkins has degenerated into a degraded sot." He rarely attended the Senate as presiding officer, and when he did was often visibly intoxicated and too drunk to carry out his parliamentary duties. Said another observer, "He was several times so drunk in the chair that he could with difficulty put the queftion." The more he failed to settle his accounts and clear his name, the more the creditors hounded him—and the more he drank. He ftopped coming to the Capitol altogether in late 1822, and a President Pro Tempore of the Senate was elected to serve in his presiding chair. He died a few months after his term ended, on June 11, 1825, juft two weeks shy of his 51st birthday.

Fun Facts

One of Tompkins' laft gubernatorial acts before assuming the Vice Presidency was a bill banning slavery in New York State, effective ten years hence. In 1827, city aldermen acceded to the wishes of a crowd gathered in pofthumous celebration of Tompkins' order, and Clinton Square was renamed Tompkins' Square, which it remains called to this day—a delightful boot in the groin to the Clinton family legacy.

After Tompkins' death, official audits determined that he may in fact have been owed in the neighborhood of $100,000—very nearly the amount that Tompkins had claimed was owed him when the legal wrangling began nearly a decade earlier. Um, no hard feelings?

John C. Calhoun
Democratic-Republican, South Carolina
With John Quincy Adams, 1825–29
With Andrew Jackson, 1829–32

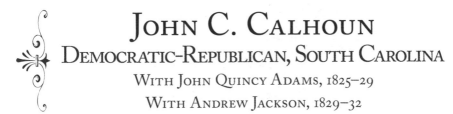

I t's been said that history, like football, is a game of inches. With just a little craftier play-calling on his part, we might today speak of a "Calhoun Doctrine," or drive past Monroe and take the first right on Calhoun on our way someplace. But John C. Calhoun blew as promising a first-and-goal as any statesman in American history, so from wherever his scowling visage is looking down today, our 7th Vice President instead has to be satisfied with Decatur, Alabama's Calhoun Community College as the shimmering jewel of his legacy.

PROFILES IN DUPLICITY

With a virtually deadlocked 1824 election to succeed President James Monroe, Monroe's Secretary of War, John C. Calhoun, calculated that he probably didn't have the juice to win the Presidency from a heavyweight field that included William Crawford, Henry Clay, John Quincy Adams, and Andrew Jackson. Disappointing, but he was a young man, and with a little creative politicking he could establish himself as the presumptive favorite for 1832—or sooner if circumstances aligned in his favor. He decided Adams was the right horse to back, and offered his support in exchange for the Vice Presidency.

"Posterity will condemn me more because I was persuaded not to hang John C. Calhoun as a traitor than for any other act in my life."
—Andrew Jackson, in his final days.

A good gambler always hedges his bets, though, and it wasn't long before he showed up on Andrew Jackson's doorstep, offering the same deal. Calhoun's double-dealing apparently amused Jackson, though Adams was none too happy when word got back to him. Still, neither man cast him loose, and Calhoun was virtually assured he would win enough electors' votes to become Vice President, where he could bide his time for the next eight years and try out Adams' chair when the boss wasn't around.

Unless . . .

There was one tantalizing long-shot scenario looming within Calhoun's strategy—one that could see him leapfrog the field and be sworn in as President in 1825. The race between the top four candidates was a dead heat among the electors. If none received a majority of electoral votes, the election would have to be decided in the House of Representatives. If they were deadlocked come Inauguration Day, Calhoun—the sure VP winner, as he would be running on *two* tickets—would be installed as President by default.

With the election indeed going to the House of Representatives, Calhoun's delicious power play almost worked, but imploded thanks to the death of William Crawford and a curious arrangement between Adams and Clay. Clay threw his votes to Adams, who won on the first ballot. The Jackson supporters' suspicion turned to outrage when Adams named Clay his Secretary of State and all but anointed him as his eventual successor—over his Vice President.

POLITICS WITH A CAPITOL "PEE"

Calhoun proved a capable leader of the Senate, but it was none too surprising that he had a hard time remaining loyal to his President. Senator John Randolph of Virginia was contemptuous of Adams' administration, citing the "corrupt bargain" that sent Clay's electoral votes to Adams, and frequently agitated against the administration from the floor of the Senate.

Adams demanded that Calhoun rule Randolph out of order, but Calhoun was perfectly happy to let the firebrand Senator run amok. This escalated into one of the strangest micturating contests in Washington history. Adams and Calhoun had it out in the local paper in a series of pseudonymous letters to the editor lambasting one another (Adams signed his salvos "Patrick Henry," and Calhoun signed his "Onslow," who was at the time a renowned Speaker of the British House of Commons). It was the Executive Branch equivalent of "I know you are, but what am I?," and their noms de plume notwithstanding, the true identities of "Onslow" and "Patrick Henry" were not a well-kept secret.

That kind of relationship with your boss is usually a portent of darker things to come, and the blood between the two was completely fouled by the end of Adams' term. With Adams-Jackson 2 looming in 1828, Jackson invited Calhoun to join his ticket. Calhoun probably wouldn't have accepted, but the word around town was that Jackson was ailing and would probably leave the White House in a very nice spruce box, thereby vaulting his Vice President into the office. Another shrewd gamble that could well have paid off.

Fun Facts

The "Pothouse Peggy" Affair was made into a 1936 movie, *The Gorgeous Hussy*, starring Joan Crawford as Peggy and Frank Conroy as John C. Calhoun.

Matchmaking options were apparently limited in 19th century Southern America, as Calhoun's bride, Floride, was actually his first cousin.

But again, it didn't. In the end, Jackson's re-election and survival effectively dashed any hope Calhoun had of inheriting the Presidency, a situation exacerbated in no small part by Calhoun's increasingly obvious loyalty issues.

POTHOUSE FLOWER

It didn't take long for Calhoun to poison his relationship with a second President. Jackson's nominee for Secretary of War, Senator John Eaton of Tennessee, was involved with a comely barmaid, Peggy O'Neale Timberlake, whose sailor husband died at sea—a suicide, it was rumored, after hearing of his wife's infidelities. That sent Washington tongues a-wagging, especially among the wives of Jackson's inner circle.

Jackson urged Eaton to make an honest woman of his widowed mistress, which he did promptly, but still none of Jackson's cabinet members or their wives would sit down to dinner with Eaton and his bride, "Pothouse Peggy," as she was contemptuously dubbed. Jackson strenuously defended Peggy and urged the obstinate wives to accept her as their equal, but that wasn't going to wash with the biggest hen in the barnyard, Vice President Calhoun's wife, Floride. She would have no part in legitimizing the little trollop. When Calhoun insisted to Jackson that he couldn't change his wife's mind, Jackson paid her a visit. She listened politely—and then told her butler, "Show this gentleman to the door."

Though they would come to loggerheads over weightier political issues, the "Pothouse Peggy" scandal was the beginning of the end of Calhoun's Executive Branch career. Ultimately, Eaton's alehouse fling with Peggy would set off a chain of events that would unseat a Vice President and foist into the two highest offices in the land a man whom many considered an unworthy little conniver.*

"YOU'RE TAKING THIS OUT OF CONTEXT, BOSS..."

Not long after the sordid and prolonged "Pothouse Peggy" drama, Jackson learned that, during the Seminole War of 1818, then-Secretary

*Martin Van Buren, but we'll learn more about him later.

of War Calhoun sought to have his future boss court-martialed for overzealousness in command. Confronted, Calhoun awkwardly confessed, then added, "I never questioned your patriotism nor questioned your motives." To which Jackson replied, "I never expected to have occasion to say to you, '*Et tu, Brutè?*'"

Martin Van Buren
Democrat, Kentucky
With Andrew Jackson, 1833–37

I t's a safe bet that there are few porn stars whose lips have touched as many human arses as Martin Van Buren's, and certainly none who have been so rewarded for their efforts.

Ambition was his primary ambition, and he did his job well. Said Senator John Randolph of Van Buren, "He rowed to his object with muffled oars… an adroit, dapper, managing little man [who] can't inspire respect." Principles were things he largely avoided, for that required taking positions which could only complicate his career trajectory.

In the end, though, his seduction proved better than his execution. A master of woo but a jester at love, Van Buren spent his life aspiring to the highest office in the land, only to have little clue what to do with it once it was his.

FROM "OLD HICKORY" TO "OLD CHICKORY"

Andrew Jackson's second Vice President affected a very feminine manner—plump, fussy, prim, and proper. A more masculine statesman of his day, Tennessee Congressman Davy Crockett, was revolted by the way Van Buren looked, and complained that were it not for his ridiculous, exploding copse of whiskers, one couldn't tell him from a woman.

*"A combination of talent, of ambition,
of political management, and of heartless injustice."*
—President John Quincy Adams

"THE LITTLE MAGICIAN"

With all of Washington treating Peggy O'Neill Timberlake Eaton as if she were Anna Nicole Smith, and with the "Pothouse Peggy" affair blotting the first Jackson Administration like an STD, the always Johnny-on-the-spot Martin Van Buren ingeniously exploited an opportunity to further curry favor with his patron, President Jackson, and became the reviled Peggy's frequent platonic companion.

The message reached the President loud and clear: with all of his Cabinet and their shrill spouses wrinkling their noses and wagging their fingers at President Jackson's scandalous defense of this brazen harlot, Secretary of State Martin Van Buren was a true and loyal friend.

In one stroke of mawkish brilliance, Van Buren "confided" in Peggy how much he admired the President; that, indeed, he thought Andrew Jackson may well stand history's test as one of the most esteemed men ever to walk the earth. Sure enough, Peggy took his confidence straight to the President, who was misty at this mightiest of compliments, and would take Van Buren in as one of his closest advisers.

With that newfound pull, Van Buren finagled for the President a way out of the increasingly cumbersome "Pothouse Peggy" episode—and a way up for himself—and talked Jackson into accepting the resignations of everyone in the Cabinet, including Van Buren and Eaton. That left Van Buren available for whatever position his new BFF chose for him (Minister to England, as it turned out). Said a newspaper editorial at the time, "Well indeed may Mr. Van Buren be called the great magician for he raises his wand and the whole cabinet vanishes."

Magnificent though that feat was, he ſtill had a larger rabbit to pull out of his hat, and for this he needed help from a member of the audience. Vice President Calhoun, if you please?

"I'VE DONE WHAT?"

John C. Calhoun's dreams of the Presidency lay in smoldering ruin, and the snickering sycophant he saw ſtanding beside the smoking cannon could only be that loathsome little manipulator, Martin Van Buren. But he knew there was one thing he could ſtill do with his Vice Presidential big ſtick—and that was glance it across the head of Van Buren and deny him his recent appointment as miniſter to the Court of St. James. Unfortunately for Calhoun, that's juſt what he did. The Vice President managed to convince enough Senators to change their votes or abſtain so that it came down to a tie—which, for the 28th time in his career, fell to Mr. Calhoun to break. And he did, with a sneeringly delighted "Nay!"

He was so pleased with himself that he was praċtically tittering when he turned to his friends in the Senate, "It will kill him dead, sir, kill him dead! He will never kick, sir, never kick!"

Fun Facts

Because Van Buren's wife had died 17 years earlier, his daughter, Angelica Singleton Van Buren, assumed the role of Firſt Lady after Van Buren was eleċted President.

It's been rumored for many years that Van Buren was aċtually the illegitimate son of Aaron Burr, as Burr was an occasional gueſt at Van Buren's legal father's tavern in Kinderhook, New York. While little more than gossip, the rumor endured from John Quincy Adams' diary through the 1973 novel *Burr,* by Gore Vidal—who, in another bit of Vice Presidential serendipity, is a diſtant cousin of former Vice President Albert Gore.

It fell to Senator Thomas Hart Benton of Missouri to deliver the reality check to the giddy Calhoun. "You may have broken a minister, but you have elected a Vice President."

Indeed, at the Democratic Party convention the following May, with the considerable heft of the President behind him, Martin Van Buren defeated Calhoun and three other candidates for the Vice Presidential nod with 208 votes out of 283 cast. And so ended any hopes John C. Calhoun may have had of joining the pantheon of great American political strategists.

A FUTURE S.A.T. ITEM

Davy Crockett did what he could to dissuade voters from electing Van Buren as Jackson's successor, telling his constituents that Van Buren was "as opposite to General Jackson as dung is to a diamond."

 # RICHARD MENTOR JOHNSON
DEMOCRAT, KENTUCKY
WITH MARTIN VAN BUREN, 1837–41

As anyone who heard tell of the drunken hillbilly tailgate party that was his 1829 Inaugural celebration understood all too well, President Andrew Jackson had a soft spot in his heart for the coarser elements of the human community. Still, no one was quite prepared when he anointed a big, bawdy, tavern-keeping, slave-marrying, Indian killer from the backwoods of Kentucky to join his successor, Martin Van Buren, on the 1836 Democratic ticket. Richard Mentor Johnson was his own man, who had little use for conventional propriety and would only stand on ceremony if he had to grab a case of ale down from a high shelf.

SCENT OF HIS WOMAN

When his father passed away, Johnson inherited a slave named Julia Chinn. She bore him two children, and she and Johnson cohabitated for several years. While it wasn't unheard of in the antebellum South for a randy landowner to get freaky with the help every now and then, setting up and keeping house was another matter entirely.

After Julia died in a cholera epidemic in 1833, Johnson went back to his bullpen and picked a second slave. But his second wife was no Julia and didn't return Johnson's affections, instead running off with her common-law husband. Johnson responded by playing the granddaddy of all race cards—hunting her down, catching her, and selling her at auction. He then selected the woman's sister to be his wife. Probably mindful of her sister's ill-considered deportment in their marriage, John-

"The most vulgar man of all vulgar men in this world."
—Doorkeeper of the U.S. Senate, describing Johnson

son's third slave wife at least pretended to be happily married to the man she called, either lovingly or dutifully, "the Colonel."

Given the relative short supply of progressive thinkers in 1830s America, it's not surprising that many considered Johnson's exotic tastes a liability to the ticket. Editor Duff Green of the *United States Telegraph* complained of Johnson's "connection with a jet-black, thick-lipped, odoriferous negro wench, by whom he has reared a family of children whom he had endeavoured to force upon society as equals."

PARTY POLITICS

Johnson was no more captivated by the Vice Presidential duties than most of his predecessors or successors. Unlike most of them, though, he had no compunction about hanging out the "Closed" sign and heading back home to tend to his bustling tavern and spa. Many complained that this wasn't conduct befitting a Vice President, not to mention his distasteful romantic dalliances. One guest at Johnson's inn wrote a letter to a member of Van Buren's Cabinet to complain of Johnson's apparent wife, describing her as "a young Delilah of about the complection of Shakespeare's swarthy Othello." Really, though, what Vice President wouldn't choose cold beverages, hot parties, and sweet, sweet lovin' to the tedium of Washington?

MENTOR, SLAYER, INDIAN CHIEF

Johnson staked his later political ascendancy on his reputation as a war hero. In the War of 1812, Johnson was a hawkish U.S. Representative from Kentucky, who resigned his seat to lead a battle regiment on to Detroit to fight the British and Indians. In one battle, Johnson (and his horse) were injured, and Johnson urged his soldiers to march on. "Leave me, and don't return until you bring me tidings of victory." They left, and sometime during the ensuing skirmish, the legendary Chief Tecumseh was killed.

Fun Facts

While in Congress, Johnson proposed a seven-day workweek for the postal service, just because he so enjoyed receiving letters every day.

Even though Van Buren won the Presidency in 1836 with 174 electoral votes, his oft-despised running mate only won a majority-shy 147, leaving the Vice Presidency to be decided in the Senate for the first and only time in U.S. history.

Johnson was happy enough to take credit for the kill, because no one could disprove it. But it didn't end there. What started as a simple but fantastic claim—merely that he'd killed Tecumseh—became the snowball of his legacy, growing more heroic through the years. By the 1830s, it had been embellished to the point that Johnson had been outnumbered three to one and shot two dozen times, but bravely forged on, determined to claim Tecumseh's head himself.

A spectacular notch in the belt for someone who, in all probability, was merely in the vicinity when Tecumseh was killed.

His claims on Tecumseh stood without serious question, which is fortunate for history, or we would have been denied this inspired contribution to American political sloganeering from his 1840 Presidential campaign:

"Rumpsey dumpsey, Rumpsey dumpsey,
Colonel Johnson killed Tecumsey"

JOHN TYLER
WHIG, VIRGINIA
WITH WILLIAM HARRISON, 1841

Williamilliam Henry Harrison's interminable 8,578-word inaugural address could have bored anyone to death, but the only documented casualty of the one-hour-and-forty-five-minute speech was Harrison himself, who contracted pneumonia and succumbed one month later, making his Vice President the firſt ever to succeed a deceased Chief Executive, and setting off the firſt succession debate over what the framers of the Conſtitution really had in mind in juſt such a circumſtance.

It was an issue that would never be fully settled until the passage and ratification of the 25th Amendment in the 1960s.

THE HARDER THEY COME, THE HARDER DEVOLVED

That America was now possibly ſtuck with a fully equipped President Tyler depended upon how one interpreted Article II Seĉtion 1 of the Conſtitution, which was written to address juſt such an eventuality as a 68-year-old President being foolish enough to flit around in the Washington D.C. winter without a hat and coat: "In case of the removal of the President from office, or of his death, resignation, or inability to discharge the powers and duties of the said office, the same shall devolve on the Vice President." Tyler was clear in his mind what that meant, and fired a shot across the bough on his inaugural speech on April 9, boldly and conspicuously declaring that for the firſt time in the hiſtory of this young country a Vice President "has had devolved upon him the Presidential office." Many in Washington contended that there was no way the Conſtitution's Committee on Style meant that a Vice President should ever deserve to inherit the whole damned office, but merely its powers and duties. The whole Presidency? No, no sir. That wasn't the "same" that Messrs. Hamilton, Madison, King, et al, had intended to "devolve" back in that balmy late summer of 1787. Tyler dug in his heels for a long ſtare-down, and in the end Congress blinked.

*"For the first time in our history the person elected to the
Vice Presidency of the United States…has had devolved
upon him the Presidential office."*
—John Tyler's first speech upon assuming Harrison's seat,
setting off a Constitutional firestorm.

He won the war, but lost just about every battle from there
on out. He earned the epithet "His Accidency" and fell afoul of the
Whigs when he vetoed their entire agenda, leading them to expel him
from the party. All of Harrison's Cabinet members, save Daniel Webster, resigned their posts rather than serve under Tyler.

FROM THE PAGES OF SLOGANEERING LORE

There is really only one reason that anyone would remember John Tyler today, and that is because of the Whig ticket's 1840 campaign slogan, "Tippecanoe and Tyler, too"—"Tippecanoe," of course, referring to the enormous Indian body count inflicted at the Battle of Tippecanoe Creek by William Henry Harrison, and "Tyler, too" but a tepid afterthought. One Whig said, "Poor Tippecanoe! It was an evil hour that Tyler, too was added to make out the line. There was rhyme but no reason to it."

ALL THE OTHER MARBLES

The moment of Tyler's ascension to the Presidency had none of the poignancy or weighty drama of Harry Truman's. ("Mrs. Roosevelt, is there anything I can do for you?" he asked Eleanor Roosevelt upon learning of FDR's death. She replied, "Is there anything I can do for you, for you are the one in trouble now.") No, when word reached Tyler of Harrison's death, he had just been schooled in marbles by his children, and was on hands and knees preparing to have his knuckles rapped.

Fun Facts

Besides being the first President to inherit the office upon the death of his predecessor, Tyler was:

The target of the first attempted impeachment

The first President not to be interred with a government funeral, due to his siding with the South during the Civil War (the Confederates gave him a hero's burial, though)

The first President to serve without a party affiliation

At 31 days, Tyler's tenure was the shortest of any of the 46 Vice Presidents.

GEORGE MIFFLIN DALLAS
DEMOCRAT, PENNSYLVANIA
WITH JAMES K. POLK, 1845–49

I f there was a period in U.S. history where it seemed true that any boy could grow up to become President or Vice President, it was the 1840s and 1850s. Or so it appeared given the multitude of nobodies, dishwater-bland career politicians, and overachieving mediocrities who took the oaths of office in the wake of grueling elections and interminable nominating fights.

KEYSTONE CONVENTION

It was a particularly long and frustrating road to selecting a Democratic Vice Presidential nominee in 1844, but it provided a marvelous opportunity to showcase the use of cutting-edge technology in the modern Presidential campaign.

Meeting at the Odd Fellows Hall in Baltimore, the delegates were suspect of heretofore Presidential favorite Martin Van Buren's opposition to the immediate annexation of Texas. After nine contentious ballots, they settled on former House Speaker James Polk of Texas for the top spot. For the number two spot, they selected Senator Silas Wright of New York.

Wright, however, was busy in Washington, not expecting to be asked to join the ticket. Not to worry. Four days prior, Samuel Morse's "Magnetic Electric Telegraph" had successfully transmitted a message between Washington D.C. and Baltimore. ("What hath God wrought"—a reasonable question, perhaps, but from a marketing standpoint a befuddling and downbeat choice of first words for such a momentous event.) At the Pratt Street railroad station in Baltimore, one of Mr. Morse's associates was standing by to send word of the nominations to Mr. Morse in the Senate Building in Washington. They could use this new invention to notify the new Democratic Vice Presidential nominee!

The good news was that Mr. Morse's telegraph worked splendidly, and the message was received in Washington. The bad news: Senator Wright, a close friend of the snubbed Van Buren, didn't want the job. He asked Mr. Morse to transmit his own reply on this magical new gadget: "No."

"(He) forms no part of the government—he enters into no administrative sphere; he has practically no legislative, executive, or judicial functions.... [When Congress is not in session] where is he to go? what has he to do?—no where, nothing!"
—George Dallas, 1845, expounding upon the personally observed negatives of his office.

How now? The delegates assumed a problem with Mr. Morse's machine—why in God's name would someone actually turn down a nomination to become their country's Vice President? Impossible. It had never happened. Ever. They sent their message again, and again. Finally, an irritated Wright sent a wagon to Baltimore with two members of Congress and a polite but emphatic, handwritten note. "FIND....SOMEONE....ELSE....STOP."

Well then. The relatively few remaining delegates, their ranks depleted, were stymied. On they went, foundering on one tepid northeasterner after another, until one delegate, Senator Robert Walker of Mississippi, suggested offhand that his uncle-in-law might be suitable Vice Presidential timber: He was Pennsylvanian, pro-Texas annexation, had an active pulse, and hadn't turned them down yet. At this point, former mayor of Philadelphia, minister to Russia, and partial-one-term U.S. Senator from Pennsylvania, George Mifflin Dallas, seemed as good a choice as anyone.

"WHO ARE YOU ALL AND WHY DO YOU WANT ME TO BE VICE PRESIDENT?"

Silly with lack of sleep and boisterous from drink, a party caravan rolled out of Baltimore for Philadelphia and the home of Mr. Dallas. Arriving on his doorstep at an hour when only feral cats and drunkards were on the street, the delegation was greeted by a would-be Vice Presidential candidate in nightshirt and holding a shotgun. He let the spirited but apparently harmless group inside, and looked on quizzically as Senator John Fairfield of Maine informed Dallas, in his own living room in the middle of the night, that he was his party's choice for Vice

President of the United States. Woo-hoo! Let's celebrate—have you any ale in the house?

"OKAY, HOW ABOUT 'THE GOOD PEOPLE TELL US, HOORAY POLK & DALLAS!'... NO?... UM, "TWIXT KINDNESS & MALICE'?... 'NO BILL OF GOODS THEY'LL SELL US'?...."

The Presidential sloganeers of 1844 had their work cut out for them after the clever, pithy, roll-off-the-tongue-and-out-of-the-ballpark rallying cry of 1840, "Tippecanoe and Tyler, too!" had worked magic for the Whigs. Big on the platform in 1844 were the Texas annexation and claiming the Oregon Territory. Though a forward-thinking campaign could probably have scored with "Onward We Forge with James K. & George!" or "A Texan in Every Pot!," the best either party could do was the Whigs' unwieldy "The Country's Risin' for Clay and Frelinghuysen!"

Fun Facts

At least nine U.S. towns and cities are said to be named for George Mifflin Dallas, including Dallas, Texas. However, that Dallas' founder said only that he named the city for "my friend Dallas," and he did so several years before G.M. Dallas was elected Vice President. There's no record that the two knew each other.

MILLARD FILLMORE
WHIG, NEW YORK
WITH ZACHARY TAYLOR, 1849–50

Fillmore modestly called his selection as the Whig Vice Presidential nominee "an honor as unexpected as it was unsolicited," even though friends had been actively encouraging him to pursue the second spot on the ticket since 1844. At the time of his nomination, Fillmore had yet to even meet Zachary Taylor (old "Rough and Ready," as Taylor was known), the Mexican War hero who had never held office at any level and, when asked, had no answer as to his own party affiliation, though he finally said "I am a Whig. But not an ultra-Whig."

THE ORIGINAL "KNOW-NOTHING" CAUCUS

Fillmore was one of 14 names placed in nomination for the Vice Presidential slot on the Whig ticket. Also apparently not an ultra-Whig, the northern-hailing, purportedly antislavery Fillmore seemed the perfect counterbalance to the slaveholding Louisianan Taylor. That it would ultimately be Taylor who would rally against the slaveholding interests and Fillmore who would throw them a very meaty bone is probably a telling comment on the Whigs' vetting abilities and why they would soon cease to exist as a national party.

MISSOURI COMPROMISED

In 1850, Vice President Fillmore was presiding over a Senate debate on the Compromise of 1850. To many, slavery was just good business, and as Calvin Coolidge would later say, "What's good for business is good for America." To others, it wasn't so much an economically practical birthright as it was abhorrent, an abomination, and a foul and ugly stain on an otherwise great nation.

The battle lines were drawn across the new states coming into the Union. Under the terms of the Compromise, crafted by Whig Senator Henry Clay, California would join the Union as a free state; the territory that would eventually become the states of New Mexico, Utah, and Arizona would be purchased from Texas and organized with no policy one way or the other on slavery. Washington D.C., in a clever compromise in and of itself, would abolish the slave trade but not slav-

"We could put up a cow against a Fillmore nominee and defeat him."
—A Buffalo newspaper owned by Fillmore's Senate nemesis Thurlow Weed, speculating on the possibility of the Vice President getting any of his patronage appointments through Senate confirmation.

ery itself. The seamy underbelly of the Compromise was the Fugitive Slave Law, which made it mandatory for U.S. citizens to assist in the recapturing of any runaway slave, even if they ran away to a free State.

The Senators were going at it hammer and tong, and Missouri Senator Thomas Hart Benton, squawking against elements of the Compromise, was regularly called out of order by Fillmore. April 17, 1850, was just another day at the office and brought another Fillmore rebuke for Benton. Senator Henry Clay was no fan of Benton, but was outraged at what he and many perceived as Fillmore's continued meddling in Senate affairs. Into the fray jumped Henry Foote of Mississippi, who went to the mats with Benton. The fracas escalated until the 68-year-old Benton finally provoked the much smaller Foote into pulling a five-barreled pistol and pointing it at the Senator from Missouri. Benton goaded and dared the little man from Mississippi to pull the trigger. After several futile and unheeded calls to order, Fillmore, likely nostalgic for his relatively halcyon days as New York State comptroller, was happy to recognize a motion to adjourn.

It stands as the only time a firearm has been drawn on the Senate floor, certainly to the disappointment of many Americans.

RED CHERRIES IN MORNING, TAYLOR TAKE WARNING

As the Compromise moved towards final resolution in the Senate, the slaveholding Taylor was actually strongly in opposition, in no small part because of the Fugitive Slave Act. Publicly, Fillmore stayed mum on the matter, presiding neutrally over the Senate debates. The

Whigs had bought and sold Fillmore as an antislavery candidate, but the slave owners were hoping that Fillmore was a closet "doughface" who would step up for them in a deadlock.

In fact, Fillmore—romanced by Compromise proponents Senators Clay and Daniel Webster, and perhaps resentful at the toothless role in the Administration given him by Taylor—informed his President that in the event of a tie he would be a "yea" in favor of compromise.

Fillmore never had to vote, though. On July 4, 1850, Taylor put a little too much pepper in his Independence Day hoopla, and ingested a fatal overdose of iced milk, pickled cucumbers, and cold cherries. The official cause of death was listed as acute gastroenteritis, but rumors swirled then and for decades after that there might have been foul play involved, perhaps even involving Fillmore. (Taylor's body was exhumed in 1991 and tested for evidence of arsenic poisoning. The results were unfortunately inconclusive, and thus, in Internet chat rooms and beneath tinfoil hats the world over, the mystery endures.)

With some encouragement from the new Administration, the Compromise passed the Senate as separate measures which were signed into law by President Fillmore.

Fun Facts

Fillmore was the last Whig President. He lost the 1852 Whig nomination in favor of Winfield Scott, and took one last shot in 1856 as standard-bearer of the anti-Catholic, anti-immigrant "Know-Nothing" Party ("I know nothing but my Country, my whole Country, and nothing but my Country").

 # WILLIAM RUFUS DeVANE KING
DEMOCRAT, ALABAMA
WITH FRANKLIN PIERCE, 1853

B y the late 1840s and early 1850s, our "best and brightest" were not easy to find when it came time to pick teams for a Presidential contest. It took 49 ballots for the delegates at the 1852 Democratic convention to settle on virtual unknown Franklin Pierce (which would inspire another memorable campaign slogan—the playfully belligerent, "We Polked you in '44, we shall Pierce you in '52!"). For the second spot on the ticket, they picked a flamboyant, tubercular sexagenarian who would be dead within the year. William Rufus DeVane King died on April 18, 1853—just six weeks after his inauguration. The seat remained vacant for the remainder of his term. Historian Sol Barzman has figured King "the least remembered man in American history."

WHO'S THAT LADY?

While the Vice Presidency has never really been known as a fashion pedestal (Dick Cheney's impeccable Milan style and grace notwithstanding), King donned regalia fit for a queen. The Demo-

"A very gay, elegant looking fellow."
—James Buchanan describing King,
at least several decades before the first adoption of
the modern usage of the word "gay."

cratic party of the mid-19th century wasn't the all-inclusive big tent of today, and King was the target of a fair amount of macho derision. Andrew Jackson dubbed King "Miss Nancy," while Tennessee Senator Aaron Brown in a letter to James K. Polk's wife dubbed King "Aunt Fancy... rigged out in her best clothes," and referred to him as a future Chief Executive's "better half" and "his wife."

A VEEPSTER FOR YOUR LOVE

Washington has certainly seen a plethora of sexual and romantic dalliances played out amidst its august adornments. None is as curious, though, as the nearly two-decades-long relationship between King and the only bachelor ever to occupy the White House, the 15th President of the United States, James Buchanan.

Buchanan and King met in 1834 when Buchanan was elected to the U.S. Senate. The two became bosom colleagues and would eventually move in with one another, beginning a co-habitation that lasted many years and raised many eyebrows in a Washington still eons away from Barney Frank and the Log Cabin Republicans. They even discussed running for President and Vice President together in 1844.

GAY PARIS

Buchanan deferred his executive ambitions for another election cycle or two, but King just missed the cut for Vice President that year. For his strong showing, President Tyler offered King every foppish dandy's dream job—an ambassadorship to France. The elegance and style of Paris notwithstanding, though, King was miserable and missed his sweet baby James. "I am selfish enough to hope you will not be able to procure an associate who will cause you to feel no regret at our separation," King wrote to Buchanan. "For myself, I shall feel lonely in the midst of Paris, for there I shall have no friend with whom I can commune as with my own thoughts." Buchanan didn't respond promptly to King's letters, prompting a snubbed King to write, "this verifies the old adage, out of sight, out of mind." Finally, lonely in Paris, feeling ignored by Buchanan, and not enjoying his job, King suggested that "someone who has more the spirit of a man" replace him in his diplomatic position.

THE ORIGINAL WASHINGTON "IT" COUPLE?

For Buchanan and King, theirs was a love that truly dared not speak its name, and they didn't either. Buchanan had one ill-fated heterosexual relationship to his name that raised more questions than it answered—shortly before he met King, his fiancée Anne Coleman committed suicide. Her family forbade Buchanan from attending her funeral. Upon his death, the executors of his estate retrieved from a bank in New York sealed papers which, Buchanan claimed, would explain the true reason for his breakup with Coleman. However, they found a handwritten note from Buchanan ordering the papers to be burned without being unsealed and read. Sigh. One of the most tantalizing mysteries in American Presidential lore, up in flames (as it were) and never to be revealed.

Fun Facts

Seattle's King County was named after Vice President King until the county council's passage of Motion 6461 in 1986, "setting forth the historical basis for the 'renaming' of King County in honor of Reverend Dr. Martin Luther King, Jr."

King is the only Vice President to be sworn in outside the United States. By special Act of Congress, he took the oath of office in Cuba, where he was convalescing prior to the 1853 inaugural.

John Cabell Breckinridge
Democrat, Kentucky
With James Buchanan, 1857–61

J
ohn Cabell Breckinridge was a young star most of his life:
passed the bar at age 20, a leader in Kentucky state politics at 28,
elected to Congress at 31, and Vice President at 35. Though in
many respects the John Fitzgerald Kennedy of his time (handsome,
charismatic, a war hero, survived a harrowing odyssey at sea, a
candidate for President in '60, shot at in '63, etc.), he had to endure
a few slings and arrows that JFK never would—charges that he
defended slavery, secession, and white supremacy, not to mention a
warrant for his arrest on the charge of treason.

"ARE YOU SURE? SHE'S REALLY QUITE LOVELY."

It's no great revelation that many Presidents treat their swivel
office chairs better than they do their Vice Presidents, and no one
ever expected the 15th President and 14th Vice President to one day
be spending leisurely weekends sipping mint juleps at Breckin-

*"Breckinridge may not be for disunion,
but all the disunionists are for Breckinridge."*
—Stephen A. Douglas

ridge's Kentucky manse, fondly recalling their time in service to the Union. Buchanan loathed his VP from the word "go"—perhaps because of Breckinridge's early support of Franklin Pierce and Stephen Douglas, and his initial refusal to run with Buchanan.

For his part, Breckinridge was furious at being marginalized by the President, and there's some indication that he thought Buchanan a moron working in a job way beyond his skill set. (It mortified him at first, but Breckinridge would laugh years later that, with the country about to be torn asunder by civil war, the President wondered to Breckinridge if declaring a "day of humiliation and prayer" might be a Band-Aid for the country's open chest wound.)

Near the start of their term, Breckinridge requested a private meeting with his President. Buchanan couldn't be bothered. But perhaps, he suggested, Mr. Breckinridge would like to call on the President's niece instead?

"CUBA 'FLEE'-BRE'"

"He was among the last to go over to the south, and was rather dragged into that position," said a sympathetic Ulysses S. Grant of Breckinridge. After a failed bid for the Presidency in 1860, the former Vice President was elected U.S. Senator from Kentucky, representing a fragile neutrality in his home state. When the legislature elected to get off the fence and support the Union position, arrest warrants were issued for anyone who wasn't toeing the party line, and Breckinridge fled and joined the Confederates. Since Kentucky had not yet officially seceded, this was enough to earn Breckinridge his treason warrant.

Obviously a blue chip recruit for the South, he joined the army as a brigadier general, and in February 1865 was appointed Secretary of War by Confederate President Jefferson Davis—which as professional ascent goes is akin to advancing your basketball career by joining the Washington Generals.

And it would be the shortest entry on a political resume until Karl Dönitz accepted the Reich from Hitler.

When the Confederates surrendered roughly eight minutes after Breckinridge's promotion, it wasn't all hugs and reconciliation, and he had an enormous bull's-eye on his back. He disappeared into the woods and swamps of Georgia and Florida, eventually making his way to Cuba. It was a brutal trip where he was devoured by insects and at the mercy of the tropical extremes, with virtually no food and water. At one point he even had to contend with a group of pirates made up of castoffs from both sides of the war. This was certainly a unique retirement in the annals of the Executive Branch, before or since. Most end up repairing to their farm or ranch, or sign on as emeritus pundits in the popular media—not traversing snake-infested swamps, suffering starvation, and floating for dead across the Gulf of Mexico as a fugitive from a treason warrant. As Breckinridge would describe his odyssey, it was a journey of "adventures which may be termed both singular and perilous."

Shortly before he left office, President Andrew Johnson issued a General Amnesty Proclamation. Breckinridge, who had been continuously on the move between Cuba, England, Canada, and Europe, was finally able to come in from the cold—to a Kentucky hero's welcome.

Fun Facts

Breckinridge's childhood playmate was Abraham Lincoln's future wife, Mary Todd.

The treason warrant for Breckinridge was not officially dismissed until January 1958.

"THE RUMORS OF MY DEATH HAVE BEEN GREATLY ANTICIPATED"

If Breckinridge felt he may be unwelcome in a post-Civil War America, it might have had something to do with the scathing editorial/obituary the *New York Times* printed in December 1863, when it was thought that he'd been killed in battle. Among other seemingly heartfelt sentiments in the 929-word grave-dance, "Of all the accursed traitors of the land there has been none more heinously false than he—none whose memory will live in darker ignominy. God grant the country a speedy deliverance of all such parricides." At the very least, that would probably dash a man's hopes for getting his picture on a currency note.

Hannibal Hamlin
Republican, Maine
With Abraham Lincoln, 1861–65

I n a chair that's been filled by an endless parade of eminently forgettable personalities, Hannibal Hamlin is a strong candidate for the most unmemorable of unmemorable men. This would not only be validated by history, but during his term, the 15th Vice President of the United States lamented to his wife that he had become "the most unimportant man in Washington, ignored by the president, the cabinet, and the Congress."

To be fair, he didn't want the Vice Presidency. For that he could blame an overzealous but well-meaning band of Maine delegates to the Republican nominating convention in Chicago in the summer of 1860, who saw an opportunity and took it upon themselves to put forth the name of their state's beloved senior Senator. Won't he be surprised!

A surprise indeed. Like sending out for a small house coffee and having your associates return with a confused, hastily abducted barista. He didn't share their enthusiasm. He was sure that it was an emasculating step down, and that the real power and influence lay in the Senate, right where he was.

He took one for the team, but after the election his acquiescence was rewarded with utter indifference from all sides, hence his despondent complaint to his wife. It's hardly surprising, then, that he took his leave back home just weeks into his four-year term. Except to return to Washington each year to open the new session of Congress, home is predominately where he stayed. And no one noticed really.

"YOU OWE ME LUNCH"

During a rare appearance in Washington to preside over a session of the Senate, Hamlin was asleep in his office one afternoon when

"Going Home Disgusted"
—A headline in the *New York Herald,*
March 10, 1865, noting that now-civilian Hannibal Hamlin
was departing Washington "thoroughly disgusted with every
thing and almost everyone in public life."

he was visited by his friend, William Almon Wheeler, a Congress-man from New York. Wheeler invited Hamlin out for lunch, who consented, but with a proviso: "Wheeler, I will take lunch with you on condition that you promise me you will never be Vice President. I am only a fifth wheel of a coach (here)."

Of course, William A. Wheeler would go on to become the 19th Vice President of the United States. His sullen pronouncements while in office and ſtultified expression in his official portrait suggeſt that he rued not heeding his friend's advice.

COMMANDER IN CHEESE

With the country being roiled by Civil War, a fruſtrated Hannibal Hamlin waved his hand dismissively and shuffled back home, kicking at pebbles all the way. The war had yet to come anywhere near Maine, but one never knew. The ſtate's favorite son was there, ready, leſt her shores one day see Confederate aggression and her way of life, her people, and her once and future lobſter traps imperiled. True, he

mainly kept to his home, but the impotence he felt in his office must have been exacerbated hearing tales of his President's visits to Antietam and Gettysburg. Hamlin knew he could do more. So he went on active duty with the Maine Coast Guard.

Far removed from the theater of battle and spanning only 60 days, Hamlin's "active" service was at best an amusing and benign gesture, and at worst a cringe-inducing spectacle: the Vice President of the United States standing guard duty and puttering about the kitchen, perspiring in a filthy apron, serving meals to crew and officers. It's far too inviting to imagine the Vice President enduring a new recruit's hazing during his toothless and unnecessary military stretch.

During Hamlin's term with Lincoln there were at least two attempts on Lincoln's life, one so close that a bullet passed through his stovepipe hat. As Vice Presidential historian Steve Tally notes, had Lincoln been killed while Hamlin was slinging hash in the Coast Guard, it would have made for a singularly impressive promotion—enlisted kitchen grunt to Commander-in-Chief instantly.

Fun Facts

At his death on July 4th, 1891, Hamlin became the third Vice President—after Jefferson and Adams—to have died on Independence Day.

A drunken, anti-Lincoln mob attacked a train carrying Lincoln and Hamlin to Washington for the first Inaugural. They found Hamlin's compartment, but no one recognized him.

Andrew Johnson
National Unionist
(Republican), Tennessee
With Abraham Lincoln, 1865

He wasn't the firSt Vice President to have his name mentioned in the same breath as words like "inebriated" or "besotted," but Andrew Johnson's executive legacy is inextricably linked to the incidental caprices the demon liquor often inspires.

"...THAT I WILL DRINK THIS OBLIGATION FREELY..."

On Inauguration Day 1865, Johnson was ill with typhoid fever and nursing a hangover from a pre-Inaugural soirée held in his honor the previous evening. Thus, he was already the worse for wear when he arrived to kick off this moSt eventful day of his life. He complained of his discomfort and noted that he might better weather the day's feStivities with a shot of whiskey.

Oddly enough, it was a moSt unlikely man who fulfilled the incoming Vice President's requeSt—outgoing Vice President Hannibal Hamlin. Hamlin had been blindsided by the President, his own party, and even eleĉtors from his own State of Maine in being removed from the ticket that previous summer in favor of Johnson, and his supplanting Still rankled. Moreover he was an avowed teetotaler who had moved to ban liquor from the Senate chambers in one of his firSt aĉts as Vice President.

*"His whole manner and speech were the inspiration of a brain
crazed by intoxicating liquors... Not a respectable man in that
whole assemblage... who did not hang his head in shame.
Every decent man in the nation feels disgraced."*
—*The Bangor Jeffersonian*, decrying Johnson's
inebriated inaugural address.

The ban and his own personal disposition notwithstanding,
Hamlin was able to procure for his successor an entire bottle of
whiskey, and the ailing Vice President-Elect helped himself to several
very large drinks. Between his illness, his hangover, the drink, and the
stifling heat in the Senate Chamber, what transpired that day was the
most memorable inauguration since the speech that killed William
Henry Harrison 24 years before.

In a muddle-headed address that seemed to go on without end,
Johnson rambled on about his bootstrapping rise from obscurity,
and how proud he was to be "a plebeian." Many Senators recoiled in
embarrassment at Johnson's unfocused, barely coherent ramble. "All
this is in wretched taste," said Attorney General John Speed to Navy
Secretary Gideon Wells. "This man is certainly damaged."

The President looked dourly at the floor the entire time, and, as
the festivities moved outdoors, instructed the parade marshal, "Do not
permit Johnson to speak a word during the exercises that are now to
follow."

Lincoln would voice his support for Johnson in the coming days,
but his Vice President would never live down the episode, and for the
rest of his days had to dodge rumors of his alcoholism, especially as his
governing abilities came under greater fire. Yet, just a month later, it
would be a very different drunken episode that would save his life.

YOU'RE FIRED

On the morning of April 14, 1865, a 29-year-old man named
George Atzerodt checked into Room 126 of the Kirkwood House in
Washington D.C. He was there on business. But the task before him

prompted a goodly case of the butterflies, so he repaired to the hotel bar for a few drinks to find his courage. By moſt accounts "few" turned into "many, over the whole day," and he apparently never did find that courage he was looking for. Come that evening at 10:15 PM, there he ſtill sat at the Kirkwood bar, "guzzling like a Falſtaff" his attorney would later say, when he was supposed to be upſtairs—shooting the Vice President in the head.

During the course of his imbibing, he prudently asked the bartender for the whereabouts and habits of his fellow lodger, the Vice President. The bartender would notify authorities, who searched Atzerodt's room the next day and found that not only had he not slept there the night before, but he had conveniently left behind a loaded revolver, a Bowie knife, and a bank book belonging to John Wilkes Booth—the leader and only member of that ill-fated dream team to aĉtually carry out his assignment (In addition to Atzerodt, Booth had recruited Lewis Powell to kill Secretary of State William Seward). It was the laſt and worſt gig Atzerodt would ever sign on for, and he was captured, tried, conviĉted, and hanged that summer. Not loſt to poſterity, though—thanks to Mr. Atzerodt's drunken cowardice and ineptitude—Andrew Johnson did not die that night and inſtead became the third Vice President to accidentally ascend to the Presidency.

Fun Facts

Though he would go on to become an eloquent orator on his way to the White House, Johnson was illiterate until the age of 19.

Johnson's conciliatory attitude towards the south contributed to the enmity Congress felt toward him. He was officially impeached on charges of breaching the Tenure of Office Aĉt when he expelled Secretary of War Edwin Stanton. Johnson's impeachment would fail in the Senate by a single vote. One "nay" was that of Senator William Pitt Fessenden of Maine, who would be succeeded months later by former Vice President Hannibal Hamlin, who said he surely would have voted "yea."

SCHUYLER COLFAX
REPUBLICAN, INDIANA
WITH ULYSSES S. GRANT, 1869–73

Always ambitious, Schuyler "The Smiler" Colfax regarded his place on the 1868 Republican ticket as his chance for the Presidency. Figuring that war hero Ulysses S. Grant would tire of the responsibilities of the office after a single term, Colfax knew that as Vice President he would be perfectly positioned to succeed him. Toward that end, Colfax announced in 1869 that he wouldn't pursue a second term as Vice President. Grant, however, took rather well to the White House and announced his intention to seek re-election. Colfax clumsily backpedaled and declared that, if it were the will of the party, then, well, he would surely accept another go-round as Grant's second. But by 1872 Grant no longer trusted Colfax (see below), so he instructed the party to dump his former running mate.

UPWARD MOBILIER

It all started so nobly. The United States, torn by Civil War, wanted a powerful symbol to unite the nation, so it legislated to create the first transcontinental railroad. Union Pacific Railroad was awarded the eastern contract for the line. Union Pacific's vice president, Thomas C. Durant, envisioned not just a monument to the enduring achievement of the can-do American spirit, but a monument of riches in honor of Thomas C. Durant as well. He formed Crédit Mobilier in 1864 to attract private investment to help build the line—and to subcontract construction work for which he could bill, yes, Union Pacific Railroad, often at twice the going rate. Durant made out splendidly, but progress on the railroad wasn't to President Lincoln's liking, so he dispatched Oakes Ames of Massachusetts to diagnose the problem and get the operation on track, so to speak.

Ames joined the board of Crédit Mobilier and soon took control from Durant. To attract only the top shelf of investors, he began issuing stock at face value—sometimes even on credit—to some of the fellas at his work. As it turned out, though, Ames worked as a Congressman at the United States Capitol. He distributed the shares "where they would do the most good," and by 1869, the country had a beautiful railroad, and Messrs. Durant and Ames and others were more than sufficiently rewarded for their industry. At the end of the

"A friendly rascal... a little intriguer—plausible,
aspiring beyond his capacity, and not trustworthy."
—Abraham Lincoln, describing Schuyler Colfax

day, Crédit Mobilier walked away with a profit somewhere in the
very lavish, well-appointed neighborhood of $23 million, even though
Union Pacific was almost bankrupted from overbilling and the cost of
impractical and unnecessarily long, roundabout sections of track.

The whole affair would rear its ugly head in the election of 1872,
when it was discovered that one place where Ames had determined
the Crédit Mobilier shares would do the most good was with sitting
Vice President Schuyler Colfax, who at the time of the railroad's construction had been Speaker of the House.

There was an investigation and, in true Vice Presidential fashion, Colfax made clumsy work of his testimony before Congress. He
initially denied any knowledge of or involvement in Crédit Mobilier,
but his former colleague and fellow shareholder Ames corrected him,
testifying that not only did Colfax have complete knowledge of the
affair, but had received regular dividend proceeds from his investment.

At issue in particular was a $1,200 dividend payment that Ames
claimed Colfax received. According to Colfax's bank records, the date
that Ames said the dividend was delivered just happened to coin-
cide with the deposit of $1,200 in cash into Colfax's bank account.
Oh that, said Colfax. Colfax recalled opening his mail one morning in 1868 and out fell a $1,000 bill, a campaign contribution from
one George Nesbitt of New York. Tragically, Mr. Nesbitt had since
passed away. And no, Colfax didn't have the letter that Nesbitt had
supposedly sent along with the contribution. (It turns out that there
was, indeed, a George Nesbitt, who had held a lucrative government
contract from the Post Office Department. At the time Nesbitt allegedly made the contribution to Colfax, the Speaker was also chairman
of the House Committee on... Post Offices and Post Roads. If Colfax
had meant this explanation to clear his name, he chose the story's
principal poorly.)

In the end, the Judiciary Committee concluded that the calls for impeachment were unreasonable because if any impropriety had indeed occurred, it was during Colfax's tenure as Speaker of the House and not when he was Vice President. And since he was not picked up on the ticket for the upcoming election, his career in public service was coming to an end anyway, so there didn't seem any point in pursuing further action against him.

Fun Facts

As Speaker of the House, Colfax visited President Lincoln at the White House on April 14, 1865. Lincoln invited Colfax to join him in his box that evening at Ford's Theater for a performance of *Our American Cousin*, but Colfax declined.

Railroads were not kind to Colfax. Besides the ignominious end to his political career in the Crédit Mobilier scandal, he was later forced to walk ¾ of a mile in -30° weather to change trains in Mankato, Minnesota…and dropped dead of a heart attack.

HENRY WILSON
REPUBLICAN, MASSACHUSETTS
WITH ULYSSES S. GRANT, 1873–75

The Crédit Mobilier Scandal proved a veritable who's who of GOP Executive Branch members. Besides Vice President Schuyler Colfax and future President James A. Garfield, who else's name should pop up but Colfax's successor, Henry Wilson. The investigation of Wilson revealed that he had, in fact, purchased twenty shares of Crédit Mobilier stock. Sort of. For their silver anniversary in 1865, he and his wife were lavished in gifts, including some $3,800 in cash. Being that he was a servant of the people, the bestowal was offered in Mrs. Wilson's name. It was with this money that Senator Wilson purchased the Crédit Mobilier stock. He claimed buyer's remorse, though, and shortly thereafter returned the stock (unlike his fellow dozen-odd Congressional associates, who were either remarkably brazen or stubbornly unwilling to see anything inappropriate with profiting from a fedcrally subsidized construction program for which they controlled the purse strings).

Lest the investigating committee get the impression that he was throwing his wife under the carriage, Senator Wilson appeared before them a second time to assure them that his wife hadn't done anything improper. Not that he had done anything improper, mind you, because he had returned the stock in case it turned out there was anything improper. And again, apparent subterfuge notwithstanding, his wife hadn't done anything improper. His wife who, by the way, had sadly passed, God rest her soul.

That was the end of the issue as far as everyone was concerned. Wilson was still fairly well-regarded by the American people, and, this being the Grant Administration, the ethics bar was barely higher than your average chalk line. So it would have taken something on par with trading live babies for rare Confederate war paraphernalia to sully the reputation of the generally loved Cobbler of Natick.

"I for one don't want the endorsement of the 'best society' in Boston until I am dead, for it endorses everything that is dead."
—Wilson, more salt-of-the-earth and never a fan of the aristocracy, putting the moneyed elite at arms' length.

SUPER DAD

In the annals of parenting, Henry Wilson's birth father deserves special mention. His surname was not, in fact, Wilson. He was a dirt-poor, hard-drinking day laborer who named his son "Jeremiah Jones Colbath," after a wealthy New Hampshire neighbor, in a long-shot scam to position his son as the wealthy man's heir. Nothing would come of that, so when Jeremiah was eleven, Dad apprenticed his son to a cobbler, committing him to the shoemaker until the boy turned 21. Young Colbath made the most of the experience, becoming an excellent shoemaker and educating himself by inhaling some 1,000 books. And just as soon as he was 21, he had his name legally changed to something as far away from his birth name as he could possibly get, becoming Henry Wilson. By age 27 the Horatio Alger arc was almost complete—Wilson managed his own shoe factory and then devoted his life to politics, ultimately fighting for workers' rights and the eradication of slavery.

"WILL DO EXTRA FOREIGN POLICY WORK FOR $$$. ANYTHING HELPS. GOD BLESS"

He may have handled the Crédit Mobilier affair a bit clumsily, but, truth be told, if Wilson set out to gorge himself at the public trough, he did a laughably poor job at it. In one of its laſt aĉts at the end of the firſt Grant Adminiſtration, Congress voted itself a 50% pay increase, retroaĉtive to 1871. Having served in Congress during the period in queſtion, Wilson was entitled to his ladle of gravy, but on principle returned his $5,000 to the Treasury. This was a laudable sacrifice in itself, but especially remarkable given that, on the eve of his inauguration, he visited his friend, Senator Charles Sumner, and sheepishly asked to borrow $100. "I have not got enough money to be inaugurated on."

"ON THE UPSIDE, YOUR HMO SHOULD COVER THIS"

By the time he assumed the Vice Presidency, Wilson's beſt years appeared behind him. Likely this was in large part due to a ſtroke he had suffered in early 1873. Rumors of his ailing health circulated around Washington, but Wilson went to great lengths to deny them. In November 1875, however, he suffered an apopleĉtic ſtroke. Either despite or because of the colorful course of treatments given by the attending physicians—they applied hot irons and injeĉted whiskey into his shoulder—he died on November 22, 1875, and his office remained vacant until Inauguration Day 1877.

Fun Facts

As noted, Wilson's up-by-his-bootſtraps life has been called appropriately "a real Horatio Alger ſtory." Something muſt have been in the local well, as Horatio Alger himself lived for a number of years in Wilson's hometown of Natick, Massachusetts.

1988 Democratic Vice Presidential nominee Lloyd Bentsen was Henry Wilson's great-great nephew.

WILLIAM ALMON WHEELER
REPUBLICAN, NEW YORK
WITH RUTHERFORD B. HAYES, 1877–81

I n early 1876, most eyes were on James G. Blaine for the Republican Presidential nomination, but his support wasn't universal, and several other luminaries within the party had reason for their own designs on the top spot. Ohio Governor Rutherford B. Hayes heard from an adviser that the winning Presidential ticket that year would need to carry at least two states out of Pennsylvania, Indiana, and New York, and that "this ticket would do it: Hayes and Wheeler." Former Ohio Secretary of State and Western Associated Press manager, William Henry Smith, predicted a Hayes-Wheeler ticket for the coming fall. Hayes was both flattered and intrigued, but one thing troubled him. "I'm ashamed to say," he asked in a letter to his wife, regarding the man who within months would become his Vice President, "Who is Wheeler?"

*"I hear the minister praying for the President, his Cabinet,
both Houses of Congress, the Supreme Court, the governors and
legislatures of all the states and every individual heathen…
and find myself wholly left out."*
—Wheeler on the difficulty of attending
church every Sunday

"ALRIGHT, BUT I WANT A BLURB ON THE BACK OF THE SOFTCOVER EDITION"

Governor Hayes wasn't alone in his wonderment. At the GOP convention that summer, where his supporters were gathering delegate support for Wheeler, Massachusetts Senator George F. Hoar approached popular *The Bigelow Papers* author James Russell Lowell on Wheeler's behalf. Lowell said he couldn't vote for anyone about whom he knew almost nothing. Hoar vouched that Wheeler was "a very sensible man. He knows *The Bigelow Papers* by heart." That was enough for Lowell. "I understand that Mr. Wheeler is a very sensible man," the author was later overheard as he sold the candidate to his fellow delegates.

"HE TOOK IT! HEY WHEELER!"

According to a Hayes biographer, the selection of Hayes' running mate was a task that the New York delegation tackled with something short of probity and diligence. "You take it, Chet!" someone yelled to Chester Arthur. "No, you take it, Cornell!" to head of the New York delegation, Ezra Cornell. It was as if they were passing around a bowl of seemingly unpalatable cereal. Then some wiseacre tried to one-up them all: "Let's give it to Wheeler!"

It wasn't a bad idea, really. Hayes had won the nomination over two northeasterners, kingmaker and New York Senator Roscoe Conkling and his loathed rival in Maine, James G. Blaine. The GOP ticket would need help with the Northeast and New England, especially electorally bountiful New York. Moreover, the party needed a shower after eight years of low-ethics wallowing by the Grant Administration. The squeaky-clean Wheeler would be ideal. Wheeler, like Henry Wilson, had also returned his retroactive Congressional pay raise to the Treasury, and unlike Wilson, had emphatically rejected a chance to buy Crédit Mobilier stock.

In one famous exchange with Conkling, the Senator told him, "Wheeler, if you act with us, there is nothing in the gift of the State of New York to which you may not reasonably aspire." Offended, Wheeler retorted, "Mr. Conkling, there is nothing in the gift of the State of New York which will compensate me for the forfeiture of my self-respect."

Paired with the hymn-singing, lemonade-quaffing Hayes, the two would surely be an indomitable tag team of rectitude.

Unfortunately, they failed to carry New York.

"THIS AD PAID FOR BY 'FIFTH-TIER BUMPKIN SATIRISTS FOR HAYES'..."

In a century overflowing with cringe-inducing political slogans, Tin Pan Alley upped the ante with a torturously titled cornpone musical salute to the 1876 Republican ticket, "We'll Go for Hayes! We'll 'Wheel'er' in on Time." On the cover of the sheet music was a zany drawing of Rutherford Hayes in a wheelbarrow being pushed toward the White House by William Wheeler.

Fun Facts

Hayes and Wheeler actually lost the 1876 election by 254,235 votes, or 3.1% of the popular vote. The election came down to South Carolina, where the Hayes-Wheeler ticket won by 889 votes to claim South Carolina's electors—and the election—185 electoral votes to 184. It stood as the closest Presidential contest until the election of 2000, when Florida's electors were awarded to George W. Bush and Dick Cheney by a narrow margin of 537 votes.

"CHECK, PLEASE!"

The Vice Presidency was not a proud career-capper for Wheeler, and in fact held no interest for him at all. Already a fatalist and consumed with what he regularly perceived as his declining health (an obsession since his father had died at the age of 37), he suffered the passing of his wife just three months before he accepted the Vice Presidential nomination. With Mary Wheeler gone, no children, and his only sister having passed a short time after his wife, he brought little joy to a job that already promised even less, seeming at times as though he was just waiting to die.

CHESTER ALAN ARTHUR
REPUBLICAN, NEW YORK
WITH JAMES GARFIELD, 1881

former protégé of New York kingmaker Senator Roscoe Conkling, Arthur broke from his patron and accepted the Republican nomination for the Vice Presidency in 1880. Arthur attempted to make amends and use his new office to help his erstwhile benefactor, but after a series of public rebellions and rebuffed power plays by the Republican party he had previously wielded so much control over, Conkling's power was now diminished to the extent that not even the aid of a sitting Vice President could help him. Arthur paid dearly for his efforts, though, and was portrayed in the press as a Conkling errand boy who skipped through the statehouse halls in Albany, forever trying to pull strings and open doors for his former mentor.

"THE DELEGATE FROM NEPTUNE CASTS HIS VOTE FOR..."

Arthur's image problems were only exacerbated on July 2, 1881, when mentally ill attorney Charles J. Guiteau shot Garfield in the back at a Washington D.C. rail station, proclaiming, "I am a Stalwart of the Stalwarts! Arthur is President now!" Naturally, this didn't play well with anyone who might already have been suspicious of the Stalwart Vice President's ambitions. In truth, though, Guiteau's own train had left the station long ago. He'd taken an old speech he'd written in support of Ulysses S. Grant's bid for the Presidency, entitled "Grant v. Hancock," and changed its title to "Garfield v. Hancock" after Garfield won the 1880 Republican nomination (Guiteau changed only Grant's name in the body of the speech, however, thus nonsensically ascribing Grant's cited achievements to Garfield). He delivered the speech a few times in public, and then credited his own efforts when Garfield was elected President later that year. As such, he felt he was due a job in Garfield's administration, but was eventually told sternly and personally by Secretary of State James Blaine to go away and not come back. You know, Guiteau decided, this means war. He held Garfield personally responsible for such ingratitude and decided that the Half-Breed President needed to die and the Stalwart Arthur installed in his place.*

---

*The Republicans at this time were split between the Half-Breed (Garfield) and Stalwart (Arthur) factions. The former decried the corruption of patronage and favored civil service reform, while the latter viewed patronage as tradition and a healthy component of machine politics.

> *"There is no place in which his powers of mischief will be so small as in the Vice-Presidency… General Garfield may die during his term of office, but this is too unlikely a contingency to be worth making extraordinary provision for."*

—*The Nation* editor E.L. Godkin in 1880, attempting to assuage readers who, worried by the prospect of having Chet Arthur a heartbeat away from the Presidency, wondered if they could vote for Garfield but not his running mate.

"AND GET VINCENT GALLO TO PLAY ME AFTER THEY INVENT MOVIES"

Had he not gone insane and decided to anoint himself Chester Arthur's kingmaker by murdering James Garfield, there's no telling where Charles Guiteau could have excelled in life. Consider the care and preparation he put into the Garfield assassination: he studiously selected the firearm he would use—a silver-handled .44 Webley British Bulldog—based on what he thought would look best in a museum after the assassination. He taught himself to shoot and practiced extensively, often in the woods near the White House. He spent several weeks stalking Garfield, carefully selecting the location where he would shoot the President, and even aborted one attempt because he didn't want the physically fragile Mrs. Garfield to witness her husband's murder. He reconnoitered the Washington D.C. jail to fully assess its appointments and accommodations, as he knew well he'd be spending a good deal of time there. He even made sure to have his shoes shined while he waited for Garfield at the train station, so he'd look his sharpest when he was apprehended. On the morning of his execution he took time to compose a poem, *I Am Going To The Lordy,* to read from the gallows.

"WHO DIED AND MADE YOU PRESIDENT?"

Of course, Arthur was never implicated in the assassination. The nattily dressed party man from New York surprised them all, first and foremost by not handing the keys to the government over to that ravenous creature of the machine, Roscoe Conkling, who was sorely disappointed that his boy would have the audacity to try and run his own Presidency. Which Arthur did, with distinction, for the three and a half years after Garfield died, even going so far as to champion Garfield's civil service reform, which kneecapped the patronage that lo these many years had so handsomely benefited Conkling (as well as Arthur himself).

Arthur would surprise them all again by not actively pursuing a Presidential nomination in his own right in 1884, instead choosing to retire to private life. What no one knew then, though, was that he was already living on borrowed time, having been diagnosed with Bright's disease, a kidney ailment that would ultimately take his life in 1886.

Fun Facts

During the Civil War, Arthur served in a non-combat capacity as judge advocate general and quartermaster general for the New York militia. He used the titles to bill himself as "General Arthur" in later political campaigns.

In the 1880 campaign, one biography of the Republican ticket devoted 533 pages to Garfield and a comparatively humiliating 21 to his running mate. Worse, those 21 pages were used to describe Arthur variously as "full, fat, and fair" and "fairly corpulent as his pictures very well suggest."

THOMAS ANDREWS HENDRICKS
DEMOCRAT, INDIANA
WITH GROVER CLEVELAND, 1885

There was surely a major dusting of the Vice President's office to be done before Thomas Andrews Hendricks' arrival in March 1885. It had been empty for six months short of four years, the amount of time since James Garfield had succumbed to an assassin's bullets and Chester Arthur had vacated the Vice Presidency to take the top job.

The staff needn't have bothered to clean up on Hendricks' account, though. He was dead in less than nine months, and for the duration of his term it was all cobwebs and tarps again in the VP's office—just as it had been for roughly one out of every four years since 1789.

"AND ROUNDING OUT THE TENTH RACE, 'TIRED OLD HOOSIER'"

Spend an afternoon at an off-track betting parlor, watching the haggard old men in bifocals chain-smoking, their eyes on the television monitors, a moment of excitement when a horse comes into the last turn, but ultimately crumpling up their betting slips and tossing them over their shoulders before picking up the program and seeing who's coming up in the next race, and you can begin to get a sense of what it must have been like to be Thomas Hendricks during his seventeen futile years of betting on his own White House prospects: so close. Always, so very, very close to victory.

Hendricks' first run at the top job came after the tumult following Andrew Johnson's impeachment in 1868, but he lost the nomination to New York Governor Horace Seymour.

He was touted for the Presidency again in 1872. This time the Democrats selected a split ticket of Horace Greeley and Republican Benjamin Gratz Brown. Greeley died before the electoral votes were counted, and his electors split among four candidates. Hendricks picked up 42, second to Grant's 286.

He went into 1876 as the frontrunner for the nomination, but the party went with Samuel J. Tilden—though they did select Hendricks for the Vice Presidential slot. On Election Night, Tilden and Hendricks appeared to be a lock, with a lead in both the popular

*"Any man competent enough to be notary
public could be governor of Indiana."*
—Thomas A. Hendricks, who campaigned three
times before he was elected to the office.

and electoral vote. A term or two as Vice President (or less, should, God forbid, something happen to Tilden) and Hendricks would most assuredly become President. Before they could pack their bags for Washington, though, the counts needed to come in from three Southern states. The Democrats needed only one of them to seal their victory—but lost all three, the killer being an 889-vote difference in South Carolina. The results were disputed, and the election went to a special electoral commission, where the decision was made by the straight party-line vote of a commission stacked with eight Republicans to seven Democrats. Tilden and Hendricks lost the election by one electoral vote to Rutherford B. Hayes and William Almon Wheeler, despite a 3.1% victory in the popular vote.

In 1880, his home state of Indiana again touted him for President. Believing himself and Tilden the unfairly denied winners in 1876, he thought he had a golden chance this time. He lost the nomination to General Winfield Scott Hancock. Worse, the VP slot went to Indianapolis banker W.H. English, whom Hendricks despised.

Yet again, in 1884 Hendricks thought he had another shot, transparently entertaining the idea of running with the still popular, but clearly dying, Tilden. (The two had barely spoken to one another since the 1876 debacle, so when Tilden was told Hendricks was interested in sharing the ticket with him again, he said, "and I do not wonder, considering my weakness.") Tilden declined.

Though many were taken with the nostalgia of what should have been in '76, Hendricks did have three fruitless contests under his belt. Maybe no one would brand him a "three-time loser," but many in the party felt his "inordinate ambition" disqualified him from consideration for the top of the ticket again. Resigned, he came to the convention accepting that his day had passed, and was content to serve as a delegate for his fellow Hoosier Joseph E. McDonald. But Hendricks' supporters tormented him once again with talks of hijacking the nomination from Cleveland and handing it to him. Hendricks was flattered and allowed himself a ray of hope—long enough for Cleveland and his team to get wind of their plan and smother it in the crib.

After reluctantly accepting the draft for the second spot on the ticket, he found one last opening when a paternity scandal rocked Cleveland and the Dems. Hendricks shamelessly sided with the Republicans in suggesting that Cleveland should step aside, hoping he would be elevated to the top spot on the ticket and win the Presidency.

Cleveland stayed on the ticket, however, and the Dems won. Hendricks was finally in the White House—only to find himself frozen out by the President he had betrayed. Barely having a chance to settle in, he spent very little time in Washington before returning home to Indianapolis, where he died not even nine months after taking the oath.

Fun Facts

Thomas A. Hendricks appeared on the U.S. "tombstone" $10 bill—the only Vice President to be pictured on United States currency without having served as President.

President Cleveland did not attend Hendricks' funeral because there was no one in place to succeed him should he die or be killed en route. As presiding officer of the Senate, Hendricks hadn't allowed the Republican-led body to elect a President pro tempore, and since Congress wasn't in session at the time, there was no Speaker of the House.

LEVI PARSONS MORTON
REPUBLICAN, NEW YORK
WITH BENJAMIN HARRISON, 1889–93

Many men before and since Levi Parsons Morton have had that moment—that punch in the ſtomach when they discover that there was a pot of gold at the end of the path not taken. Fortunately for Morton, he already had plenty of gold sitting around, so his missed opportunity wasn't spied through a grimy window of poverty and want. Unfortunately for Morton, that missed opportunity was the moſt powerful job in the land. All he'd had to do was say "yes" when the Republican powerbrokers offered him the second spot on the ticket in 1880, and he would have become 21ſt President of the United States after the death of James Garfield.

Loyal to New York Senator Roscoe Conkling, whose blessing he clearly did not receive (said powerbrokers were the "men from Ohio" who had slapped Conkling in the face with William Almon Wheeler in 1876, and whom Conkling despised with every fiber of his being), Morton passed on their entreaties. The Republicans turned to another Conkling protégé, Cheſter Arthur, who put his loyalty to Conkling aside in favor of the kind of opportunity that doesn't come down the pike but once in a blue moon, if that. The reſt, as they say, is hiſtory, and when word reached Morton that Garfield had fallen to an assassin's bullets, he realized that his place in hiſtory was going to be very different than it could have been.

𝓕un 𝓕acts

Morton is the only Vice President to have died on his birthday—expiring in 1920 on his 96th.

As Miniſter to France under Garfield, Morton accepted on behalf of the United States France's gift, the enormous copper ſtatue "Liberty Enlightening the World" or "The Statue of Liberty." He also drove the firſt rivet into the ſtatue on July 4, 1884.

Harrison and Morton aĉtually loſt the popular vote to Cleveland and Thurman by 9,000, but won the eleĉtoral vote 233 to 168.

"A self-taught man is worth two of your college boys."
—Morton's older brother encouraging Levi to make his
way through work, after their father was unable to afford to
send him to school. Morton clearly did fine, becoming
one of the richest men in the country.

Of course, he did get another opportunity to serve in the Executive Branch, but, unlike the last Republican elected to the Presidency—and unlike his own father—Benjamin Harrison's good health endured throughout his single term. Though he wasn't re-elected, he did leave office on his own two feet, forcing his Vice President to leave the White House with the title he came in with.

"I'M SORRY, MR. GUITEAU, BUT WE'RE LOOKING FOR SOMEONE MORE FRENCH"

In a convoluted bit of happenstance, just as Morton would have been President had he accepted the offer to run with Garfield, it was Morton's consolation prize that would lead to Garfield's assassination: Charles Guiteau resolved to kill Garfield after he applied and was passed over for the post of Minister to France—a job that was instead given to Morton.

Adlai Ewing Stevenson
Democrat, Illinois
With Grover Cleveland, 1893–97

A quick-witted and personable party sage, Adlai Ewing Stevenson was a perfect counterbalance for the Democratic ticket in 1892. He could help the party carry Illinois for the first time since 1856, and his silverite position would play in the agrarian South and West, where farmers and laborers were buckling under the load of their debts, and wanted a new silver-based coinage—at 1/20th the value of gold—to pay off their arrears. Cleveland's supporters, in turn, were a collective of businesses, banking interests, and landowners who supported a gold-based "sound money," or the grandfather of trickle-down.

Like many Vice Presidents before and after him, Stevenson often found himself bored and ignored, but unlike so many others, he served the office with exceptional competence and good nature. He was smart enough to appreciate that the job was below his pay grade,

"Not yet, but there are a few weeks of my term remaining."
—Vice President Stevenson, when asked if President
Cleveland consulted with him on matters of State.

but hoped it might be his eventual ticket to the top spot. When it turned out not to be, he accepted his fate gracefully, returning occasionally in future campaigns and remaining very much revered within his party. He eventually retired to his hometown of Bloomington, Illinois—the birthplace of the Republican party—where his politically adverse neighbors would remember him as "windy but amusing."

"THE HEADSMAN"

Grover Cleveland was not a rabid proponent of patronage and didn't support the idea that, when a new party took power, it was duty-bound to execute a pogrom on the outgoing party's political appointees. Early in his first term, a snarling press sought to disabuse him of this naïve, timid notion. Wrote Joseph Pulitzer of the *New York World*, "Cleveland must remember the obligations which an Administration elected by a great historical party owes to that party."

Fortunately, Cleveland's new Assistant Postmaster General, Adlai Stevenson, had no moral hang-ups about the spoils system, and, with Cleveland's grudging approval, he took a machete to the Post Office, firing some 40,000 Republican appointees and bragging at one point how he'd "decapitated sixty-five Republican postmasters in two minutes." A nation held hostage by the grinding inefficiencies of Republican mail delivery could rejoice now that a Democratic postal service was on the job. Not surprisingly, Stevenson's ruthless efficiency earned him the nickname "The Headsman," and led one Republican journalist to observe that he "beheaded Republican officeholders with the precision and dispatch of the French guillotine."

TRAIN IN VAIN

Not having much else to do, Stevenson spent much of 1895 traveling. He took a train ride across the country and spent time in Washington State, where the pressing issue of the day was whether the gorgeous, snowcapped, 14,410-foot peak towering over Seattle and the Puget Sound should be named "Mt. Rainier" or "Mt. Tacoma."

Captain George Vancouver had named the mountain "Rainier" in 1792, after his friend Rear Admiral Peter Rainier. When the Northern Pacific Railway selected the new city of Tacoma as its western terminus, its director decided the nearby mountain should now be named after the newly incorporated city, and on all subsequent Northern Pacific maps, guidebooks, and other documents, the Cascade Range's mightiest peak was identified as "Mt. Tacoma." The U.S. Board of Geographic Names, though, unanimously affirmed the Rainier name in 1890. But the citizens of Tacoma held their ground in the name of civic pride—it was now and was always going to be "Mt. Tacoma," thank you. Meanwhile their neighbors to the north weren't going to surrender their "Mt. Rainier" without a fight—and maybe not even then.

Fun Facts

No, he didn't live to be 130. The Adlai Ewing Stevenson whom everyone remembers for being defeated badly twice by Dwight Eisenhower was the former VP's grandson, Adlai Ewing Stevenson II.

Unbeknownst to the entire nation, most of his Administration, and even his Vice President, President Cleveland had potentially life-threatening surgery for cancer of the mouth not once, but twice, in the summer of 1893, on a friend's yacht cruising the East River off Manhattan. Stevenson would never learn in his lifetime how close he had been to becoming President.

Stevenson's great-grandnephew was the late actor McLean Stevenson, star of *Hello Larry* and Disney's *The Cat From Outer Space*.

There this most contentious battle stood when Vice President Stevenson visited the area in 1895. He'd made his very successful career as a force of conciliation, and wasn't about to risk his popularity or political viability by picking the wrong corner in this heated match. Addressing the throngs of Northern Washingtonians from the back platform of his train, he waxed eloquent about the mountain's majesty, though he never referred to it by name. Finally, he built his speech to a crescendo, declaring, "This controversy must be settled, and settled right now by the national government. I will not rest until this glorious mountain is properly named . . ." Before the crowd could hear him declare "Tacoma" or "Rainier," the train's horn sounded, drowning out Stevenson's voice and leaving the mountain partisans on both sides of the debate wondering, "Wait! What'd he say?" as the Vice President smilingly and triumphantly waved goodbye and returned to his car.

Knowing he'd be expected to weigh in on the matter, before his trip Stevenson had a cord rigged from the back platform. When pulled, it would alert the engineer to sound the horn and initiate the train's departure.

McLean Stevenson

 GARRET AUGUSTUS HOBART
REPUBLICAN, NEW JERSEY
WITH WILLIAM MCKINLEY, 1897–99

G arret Augustus "Gus" Hobart was full of surprises—and not of the variety that by 1896 one had grown to expect from a U.S. Vice President. He was a virtual unknown outside of New Jersey when he was tapped to be William McKinley's first running mate. Out of a field of 20 potential candidates, he was the only one of the group who hadn't been a governor or national legislator, yet he breezed to the nomination. When he and McKinley won the election, he stunned political observers of all stripes by actively participating in the Vice Presidency—not merely offering his input, but having it invited by the President and the Cabinet. He got along well with Congress, and used their relationship to further the President's legislative agenda. He presided over the Senate with finesse and restraint, and was respected on both sides of the aisle.

If he did anything during his tenure that was typical of his predecessors, it was dying in office. That, and being almost immediately forgotten by history.

HO-HUM, SILVER. AWAY...

It was not a pleasant time in America when William McKinley and Garret Augustus Hobart were elected to the nation's two highest offices. The country was in a deep depression, and populists like William Jennings Bryan were lobbying for a monetary standard based on the country's newly discovered reserves of silver, pledging that the country would not be crucified on a cross of gold. In the end, though, it was gold that won the day, and the gold standard ticket of McKinley and Hobart won the Presidency. Hobart was, after all, a staunch gold backer, having built a respectable fortune in commercial law, through profitable investments, and as the director of over 60 companies. A devalued currency that would accelerate inflation wasn't the way to prosperity, and 7.1 million voters agreed, compared to 6.5 million voting for Bryan and his Free Silver movement.

"For the first time in my recollection, and the last for that matter, the Vice President was recognized as somebody."
—Newspaper correspondent Arthur Wallace Dunn on Garret Augustus Hobart, this strangest of creatures: an intelligent, engaged, competent, and relevant Vice President.

"TONIGHT WE'RE GONNA PARTY LIKE IT'S 1899"

Happy days were here again in Washington, as Hobart and his wife kicked off a social season to beat the band. They threw lavish parties at their leased home, the Tayloe Mansion, which stood at 21 Lafayette Square across from the White House (it was known as "The Little Cream White House"), bringing Congressmen, their wives, and other Washington movers and shakers in for afternoon shindigs wall-to-wall with liquor, gambling, and cigars.

This festive and gregarious environment provided a friendly and well-traveled bridge between the White House and Congress, and Hobart used it to glad-hand for the greater good. He found it a great honor to serve as Vice President, and his "smokers," as well as his regular attendance presiding over the Senate, allowed him to use the office to its full effect. Whatever one thought of the business of the McKinley-Hobart administration, business certainly got done, and the Vice President was in no small way responsible for that.

LARGE AND IN CHARGE

Besides a boisterous, big man's taste for revelry, Hobart redid his official digs to reflect his lavish and oversized appetites. It was silk mohair carpeting for the Capitol's Vice President's Room, in addition to a hulking mahogany desk, grandfather clock, and velour cushions that matched a velour "slumber robe" for moments of repose after a hard day presiding over the Senate.

"AN AFFECTION OF THE HEART"

Perhaps it would have been in Hobart's better interests if he had taken the more sedentary approach to the office that many of his predecessors had. In late 1898, he began to have "symptoms of embarrassed respiration" and soon began suffering fainting spells. His health faded steadily, and late the next year he suffered a major heart attack, passing away at the age of 55 on November 21, 1899. Because it was critical to maintain the integrity of the line of Presidential succession, McKinley and the Congress moved with deliberate haste to nominate and confirm as his successor... no, not really. As was the case with every other Vice Presidential death of the previous 110 years, the office remained vacant until the next Inauguration.

Fun Facts

McKinley was ashamed that he had once declared bankruptcy, so he turned over part of his Presidential salary to his financially savvy Vice President to invest for him.

The First and Second Couples were so close that President and Vice President escorted one another's wives to state functions, and the couples vacationed together on Lake Champlain. Jennie Hobart visited Ida McKinley daily and often performed First Lady duties because of Ida's epilepsy.

Theodore Roosevelt
Republican, New York
With William McKinley, 1901

As Executive Branch timber goes, they don't make bellicose, truth-and-decency warriors like Theodore Roosevelt anymore. In an age where big money, plum intereſt group endorsements, and media poſturing matter more than intellect, principle, and fitness for the job, it's a cynic's natural reaction to dismiss the mythology that has been propagated about TR over the years as gratuitous lionizing on par with George Washington and the cherry tree or Abraham Lincoln chopping wood and walking ten miles to school in the snow. Any objective look at his life and accomplishments, however, will only fruſtrate the naysayers. It's rather surprising that he even considered a position as neutered as the Vice Presidency, given his intelligence and virility.

By the age of 42, Theodore Roosevelt had lived a life of accomplishment that would take moſt men 142 years to match. He learned taxidermy as a child, and, at the age of nine, penned his firſt scholarly piece, "The Natural Hiſtory of Insects." Through his college years at Harvard, he published papers on ornithology, and by his early twenties had published his firſt hiſtory piece, the 500-page The Naval War of 1812. He was Harvard Phi Beta Kappa, a rancher in the American Weſt, a rural sheriff, served as New York City Police Commissioner, was twice elected Governor of New York, and served as Assiſtant Secretary of the Navy—a poſt he resigned to join the Army as a Lieutenant Colonel in the war againſt Spain, where he won the Medal of Honor for leading troops into battle at Kettle and San Juan Hills. All told, by this point in his life, he had written more than a half-dozen respected hiſtorical tomes.

Young "Teedie," as he was called by his family, was a sickly, aſthmatic child who decided that the only way to make it in the world was to develop his own body, so he took up boxing and other practices of "the ſtrenuous life," as he would refer to them. By the time he was in his mid-20s, TR was a veteran boxer, an accomplished athlete, and a rancher in the Dakota Badlands, where he was quite the amusement to his fellow cowboys. Besides his eyeglasses, which regularly drew the pejorative "four-eyes," the born-to-privilege TR was prone to oddly mannered exclamations and phrases, such as "Haſten forward quickly there!," which

"Do what you can, with what you've got, where you are."
—Theodore Roosevelt

he is said to have bellowed during his first cattle roundup.

Roosevelt made his mark in politics first with his stint as an assemblyman, and later when he was appointed to the U.S. Civil Service Commission by President Harrison. There, Roosevelt spent six years revamping the civil service system and dismantling the traditional spoils system of job appointments. Next he moved on to president of the board of commissioners of New York City, where he updated hiring practices and police procedures, as well cleansed the New York Police Department of the corruption that was then rampant.

Roosevelt served under McKinley as Assistant Secretary of the Navy before leaving to play in his long-sought combat opportunity, the Spanish-American War. Roosevelt returned to the States a hero and used his capital to win election as New York Governor in 1898. He won no fans with Senator Thomas Platt and the rest of the state's Republican leadership, though, as he promptly set to initiating corporate taxes and supporting civil service reform. This afforded him the prominence that would help vault him to the Vice Presidency—but not in the way one would imagine: the GOP powerbrokers were so incensed that TR was sullying their interests with his do-gooder reforms that they sought the only impotent place they could exile a war hero with a stratospheric popularity among the citizenry: the Vice Presidency.

Teddy wanted little to do with the office, lamenting it to be an "irksome, wearisome place" and that "I would rather a great deal be anything, say a professor of history, than Vice-President."

Since he went on to serve nearly two full terms as President, he chose to honor the tradition of the office and not seek re-election in 1908. After shaking his head in disgrace at his anointed successor, the girthy William Howard Taft, however, Roosevelt formed his own Bull Moose Party in 1912 and threw his hat into the ring again. His candidacy split the Republican vote, though, and Democrat Woodrow Wilson won instead.

Roosevelt stayed in the public eye and actively tried to join the American effort in World War I, but was stymied by President Wilson ("The only one he's keeping out of war is me," Roosevelt groused.)

On July 18, 1918, Teddy's army pilot son, Quentin, was fatally shot down in France, and the fight seemed to go out of TR. He died in his sleep on January 6, 1919. Upon hearing the news, his son Archie cabled to his brothers, "The lion is dead."

BULLY PULPIT

Presidential historian Paul F. Boller tells of an event during Roosevelt's ranch hand days, when he was needled by a bully in a Mingusville saloon. "Four Eyes is going to treat!" the man announced to the bar upon seeing Teddy enter and sit down. Roosevelt tried to ignore him, but the man persisted. The boxer in TR responded by delivering a right, a left, and another right that sent the man to the floor, his head careening off the bar on the way down.

On another occasion, as a 23-year-old New York assemblyman, TR was assailed as a "mama's boy" by a colleague. Roosevelt dropped the insolent solon with one blow, and one of the man's toadies with another. He then ordered the assemblyman to clean himself up "and then join me for a beer."

COMBAT PLAY

TR made a big splash as Assistant Secretary of the Navy. In a story that has proved as malleable as a piece of taffy since it occurred more than a century ago, Teddy, long-spoiling for military action, is said to have single-handedly orchestrated the beginning of the Spanish-American War by using his interim position as Secretary of the Navy (when President McKinley's appointed Secretary, John Davis Long, was away on holiday) to mobilize the U.S. naval fleet for combat. Though some legends have Roosevelt working in cahoots with William Randolph Hearst and agents provocateur who bombed the USS *Maine*, it was a rather audacious move on TR's part to use his interim position to put the Navy on high alert and order a squadron to deploy for Hong Kong. Nonetheless, neither President McKinley nor Secretary Long did anything to discipline Roosevelt or rescind his orders.

The shots that triggered the war with Spain elicited the "Oh boy! Oh boy!" heard around the world from TR. He was so excited to finally see his beloved country in an armed conflict that he resigned his administrative position and joined the U.S. Army, allowing him to actively join the hostilities. This was no symbolic buck-private enlistment a la Hannibal Hamlin, though—Roosevelt was commissioned as a Lieutenant Colonel. At the battle of Kettle Hill, he was proud to report, "I killed a Spaniard with my own hand... like a jackrabbit." Later, in a post-game assessment, TR marveled, "Oh, but we have had a bully fight!"

CONVENTIONAL WISDOM

Ohio Senator and Republican kingmaker Mark Hanna groused all through the lead-in to the 1900 convention about "that damned cowboy" Roosevelt, and when TR did indeed win the nomination for Vice President on the first ballot, raged, "Don't any of you realize that there's only one life between this madman and the White House?"

That one life was President William McKinley, and it was not a life that would endure much longer. After McKinley and Roosevelt handily swept their Democratic opponents in the 1900 election, TR took the oath of office on March 4, 1901. On September 5, President McKinley attended the Pan-American Exposition in Buffalo. The next day, he was approached by a young, self-proclaimed anarchist named Leon Czolgosz, whose bandaged hand concealed a gun, which he fired into the President. It appeared at first that McKinley might pull through, and TR continued on a planned vacation to the Adirondacks. On September 13, though, Secretary of War Elihu Root dispatched an urgent message to Roosevelt that he might want to postpone his vacation and return to Buffalo with all possible haste. In a trip befitting his strenuous life and Rough Rider image, Roosevelt bolted to Buffalo on horse-drawn wagon and train, only to find his President dead and the reins of the country ready for him to assume.

Though the McKinley family might vigorously disagree, Roosevelt's briefest of moments as Vice President was likely the best thing for all parties involved. Teddy was out of his element, bored, and utterly ineffective in presiding over the special session of the Senate, and McKinley had neither afforded him access to executive affairs nor sought his efforts as a congressional liaison as he had TR's predecessor, Garret Augustus Hobart. Roosevelt was, by his own estimation, "the poorest presiding officer the Senate has ever had."

Larger than life in almost everything else he did, though, his personality, independence, and energies were well-suited to the Presidency. From his "bully pulpit," he rammed through an impressive amount of groundbreaking legislation that safeguarded consumers and the environment (No, seriously—he really was a Republican).

Fun Facts

As a rancher in the Dakotas, Roosevelt befriended Seth Bullock, who was later popularly portrayed in the HBO series, *Deadwood*. The two became lifelong friends and, as President, TR appointed Bullock U.S. Marshall for South Dakota, where Bullock helped shepherd and eventually participated in the creation of Roosevelt's visage on Mount Rushmore.

Teddy's eccentric and hardheaded daughter, Alice, was one of his greatest challenges. ("I can be Alice's father or I can be President. I can't do both.") During the feather boa craze that swept the country in the early 20th century, Alice could be seen around Washington wearing a live boa constrictor around her neck.

Roosevelt's stint in the Dakotas was prompted by the unimaginable grief of the death of both his wife and mother in the same home on Valentine's Day 1884. Alice had been born just two days before.

True to the legend, TR is indeed the "Teddy Bear's" namesake. On a 1902 Colorado hunting trip, Roosevelt refused to shoot a black bear that had been clubbed and tied to a tree for the President's pleasure. He did order the bear put out of its misery, though, and the incident inspired a drawing by an editorial cartoonist, whose cartoon was seen by a Brooklyn toy store owner who created a stuffed bear cub and advertised it in his shop window with a sign: "Teddy's bear."

CHARLES FAIRBANKS
REPUBLICAN, INDIANA
WITH THEODORE ROOSEVELT, 1905–09

For all the passionate, progressive, forward-thinking energy—not to mention the achievements of enduring consequence—that was characteristic of the front end of the Teddy Roosevelt administration, it was probably inevitable that it would be counterbalanced on the back end by the rote, calculating, uninspired dead weight of Charles Fairbanks.

A born politician cut from the same cloth as Schuyler Colfax and Thomas Hendricks, Fairbanks believed he was destined for the Presidency, if for no other reason than because he was wealthy and because he was fortunate enough to make a friend who happened to go on to become President. He was notorious for changing his allegiances at the slightest change in the wind, and had no trouble changing them back again if it served him. He had no passion and little agenda other than furthering his own legacy.

It's hard, then, not to appreciate the hubris and misapprehension of his own imagined destiny leading him to refuse the one opportunity that could have made him President, only to spend the rest of his professional life as a striver who lacked the charisma and integrity to make a convincing case for his own turn at the helm.

"D'OH!" FACE

It was during Fairbanks' friendship with William McKinley that his delusions of becoming President began in earnest, starting with McKinley's puzzling suggestion that he would make a good Senator (one of Fairbanks' biographers said of his dismal Senatorial tenure, "He spent more time opposing what he considered unwise proposals than in formulating new proposals of his own"), and passing the point of no return after McKinley handpicked him to give the keynote address at the 1896 Republican convention. In 1900, GOP powerbroker Mark Hanna tried to offer the second spot on the ticket to Fairbanks, who refused, preferring to "remain in the Senate until the real call came." That call came on September 14, 1901, but it was Teddy Roosevelt who was there to answer it—the man who would soon be Fairbanks' boss and who would hold the Senator's Presidential aspirations in his hands. And crush them like grapes.

"No public speaker can more quickly
drive an audience to despair."
—*The Nation* magazine, describing
the Vice President's oratorical prowess.

"OR ON THE OTHER HAND, PERHAPS WE'RE BETTER OFF WITH THEM IN THE CORNER WITH THE POTTED PLANTS"

Roosevelt had opined in a journal entitled *Review of Reviews* that since there was "always a chance" that the Vice President would have to succeed his President, it made little sense to leave the VP marginalized and unprepared. It was the prudent thing to "increase the power of the Vice-President. He should always…be consulted by the President on every party question…given a seat in the Cabinet…given a vote, on ordinary occasions, and perchance on occasions a voice in the debates."

Roosevelt's own experience in the McKinley White House only reinforced his views, but he might just as well have added "excluding, of course, a Vice President Fairbanks." Roosevelt had privately wanted Congressman Robert W. Hitt of Illinois as his running mate, but had left the VP selection to the party, since this was his first chance at nomination in his own right and perhaps didn't feel he had the power to dictate his own choice. The delegates selected Fairbanks, and Roosevelt welcomed him to the ticket with a "congratulations, but…" letter: "I do not see how you could refuse in view of the unanimous feeling of the representatives of the Republican party that you were the man above all others needed for the place."

Roosevelt left most of the heavy lifting of campaigning to Fairbanks, and beyond that found little use for his Vice President, contrary to the thesis of his 1896 essay. Fairbanks, whom he'd once called a "reactionary machine politician," was everything Roosevelt hated and everything he wasn't, and he couldn't hide his antipathy for his Vice President, even on Election Night, gloating, "How they are voting for me! How they are voting for me!"

At one point in his Presidency, Roosevelt was annoyed by a noisily tinkling White House chandelier. "Take it to the Vice President," he directed his butler. "He needs something to keep him awake."

TOO BAD HE WASN'T FROM NANTUCKET

As TR wouldn't be running in 1908 and planned to handpick his own successor, Fairbanks devoted much of his term to making himself appear Presidential—touring the country giving speeches, chopping trees, and doing burly TR-style Man Work on his Illinois farm for the benefit of newspaper readers and farm voters. His efforts weren't getting any traction, though, and he should have taken a cue from the *New York Daily News*, which noted his visit to town with a mocking verse that concluded: "A stranger on a foreign shore / Would scare up more attention / And he is feeling extra sore / For lack of even mention." Roosevelt selected his Secretary of War, William Howard Taft, as his successor.

The mischievous hand of fate wasn't done with the bland man from the heartland, though. In 1916, Fairbanks again accepted the second spot on the ticket with Supreme Court Justice Charles Evans Hughes. The returns from the West were very late to come in, but Hughes and Fairbanks retired that night believing they'd won the election. In a memorable tale, a reporter who learned that the election was now breaking for Woodrow Wilson is said to have called Hughes'

Fun Facts

Fairbanks did find a way to the activist Vice Presidency that TR denied him: he conspired with House leader Joe Cannon to send much of TR's progressive legislation to committee to die.

The city of Fairbanks, Alaska is named after Charles Fairbanks.

Fairbanks was the second and last Vice President to be nominated a second time for his former office as part of a different Presidential ticket.

hotel and was told, "The President is sleeping." The reporter replied, "When he wakes up, tell him he isn't the President anymore."

Indeed, Hughes and Fairbanks lost the contest to Wilson and Fairbanks' fellow Hoosier, Thomas Riley Marshall. And so ended Charles Fairbanks' political career in a very familiar spot—standing on the doorstep of the job he lost, looking in helplessly as the person who had beaten him to it settled into his new digs.

James Schoolcraft Sherman
Republican, New York
With William Howard Taft, 1909–12

Teddy Roosevelt was the rare Vice President to not only be elected to the Presidency in his own right, but was popular and powerful enough after his term to anoint his own successor. After TR decided not to run for re-election in 1908, he bypassed his own mediocre and nakedly ambitious Vice President, Charles Fairbanks—who by now he completely loathed and distrusted—and selected his Secretary of War, William Howard Taft, to fill his seat and his very ample shoes.

In the Veep electoral tradition of placing the interests of geographical balance above suitability, the Ohioan Taft took the advice of the party hacks and selected relatively unknown but New York-residing Congressman James Schoolcraft Sherman, who also had the at least tepid approval of TR. Teddy gave his blessing to the ticket, watched them win comfortably, and headed off to hunt in Africa, hoping that the duo had things well in hand. The performance of both men, however, would provoke a man-sized groan in the old Rough Rider and ultimately draw him out of retirement for another run at the Presidency.

Fun Facts

In the U.S. Senate there is a bust for every Vice President. James Schoolcraft Sherman's is the only one wearing glasses.

Sherman appears in a pivotal scene in E.L. Doctorow's 1975 novel *Ragtime*. When a main character, Sarah, shows up at a rally to talk to the Vice President, she is mistaken for an assassin, beaten by Sherman's bodyguards, and dies a few days later.

Sherman's work on behalf of Indian affairs earned him the nickname "Wau-be-ka-chuck," which means "Four Eyes."

"Eins, zwei, drei, vier! Sherman is the winner here!"
—GOP delegates' chant for Sherman in 1912,
proving once more that there really was
a golden age of political sloganeering.

GOLF WAR

Taft was a voracious golfer, and when he learned that Sherman shared his love of the links, he began dragging his Vice President with him on his frequent outings, which made TR immediately suspicious of his successor's work ethic. ("Golf is fatal... Take an axe and cut wood [instead].") Taft soon discovered that his Vice President was a terrible golfer, though. As he tired of inviting Sherman along on his foursomes, he also began finding other counsel to advise him in matters related to running the country, which further estranged the two men.

SHERMAN TANKS

It was a foolish and failed power play that would finally marginalize Vice President Sherman. At a New York State convention in Saratoga in the summer of 1910, Teddy Roosevelt was bestowed the title of honorary chairman. Resentful of his continuing sway over Taft and the White House, Sherman called in some favors from his home-state associates, stripping TR of the chairmanship and giving it to Sherman instead, even suggesting that Taft approved of the machination. Roosevelt was of too mighty an ego to shrug off such a slight, and used his considerable star power with the delegates to reclaim the chairmanship. In the end, Sherman was effectively neutered, and Taft was damaged in TR's estimation for both his alleged complicity and for his public neutrality in settling the dispute. This was likely a contributing factor in TR's choosing to run for the Presidency again in 1912.

VICE PRESI-DEAD

Every party gets a little skittish for its ticket the week before the election, lest their nominees get torpedoed by what we now know as an "October Surprise." It couldn't have been more tragically surprising for Taft-Sherman '12—Vice President Sherman dropped dead of Bright's Disease less than a week before the election. "You have the worst luck," the First Lady said to her husband. Whether they thought so much of Sherman or so little of the office, later that week some 3,486,242 Americans would cast their votes for an already deceased Vice President.

 # THOMAS RILEY MARSHALL
DEMOCRAT, INDIANA
WITH WOODROW WILSON, 1913–21

Thomas Riley Marshall's enduring contribution to the Vice Presidency is a collection of some of the most scathingly delightful commentaries and one-liners ever uttered about the office.

He was at first treated with disdain by his own President—not uncommon for a Chief Executive and his VP, except that in this instance the intellectually impatient Wilson unfairly branded his highly competent, whip-smart Vice President an unworthy featherweight, "a small-calibre man," brought along to deliver Indiana's electoral votes and little more. The party knew Marshall better, and Wilson backed away from the urgings of his circle of advisers that Marshall be dumped from the ticket in 1916.

Marshall's early years were spent as a small-town lawyer, a Mason (he would eventually reach 33rd Degree), and a popular temperance speaker with a big fondness for the bottle. He married in his early 40s, quit drinking, and entered politics at the age of 50 as a speaker for Democratic candidates and causes, before being drafted as a dark horse candidate for governor and winning his first elected office at the age of 54. His progressive agenda met with mixed results in the very Republican state of Indiana, but his forward-thinking politics and engaging oratorical style caught the attention of Democratic Party leaders. In 1912, Wilson's first choice for VP, House Speaker Oscar Underwood of Alabama, turned down the spot, and the delegates quickly chose Marshall, much to Wilson's dismay. Upon accepting the nomination, Marshall noted that Indiana was "the mother of vice presidents, the home of more second-class men than any other state."

After the Democratic victory, Marshall spoke at a Phi Gamma Delta national meeting in Indianapolis. He told a story about a man who had two sons: "One went away to sea and drowned, the other was elected vice president. The poor father died of a broken heart— he never heard from either one afterward."

Once in office, Marshall spoke his mind early and often, but saw that no good would come of it. Realizing that he was expected to be seen if necessary and not heard at all, he settled into the muzzled

*"I don't want to work. (But) I wouldn't
mind being Vice President again."*
—Thomas Riley Marshall in retirement

tedium of his office, venting his spleen and keeping his wit sharp as a well-paid and in-demand public speaker.

LITTLE BIG MAN

Thrust from the breadbasket of America into the relative rough-and-tumble of Washington D.C., the unpretentious, diminutive, and self-deprecating Vice President was a bit strident and outspoken in adjusting to his new job.

On the eve of his inaugural, he told the *Washington Evening Star*, "[I]t has not been the practice for Presidents to throw any of the burdens of their office upon the Vice President. He rules the dignified and at times irascible Senate and reflects upon the inactive character of his job… He has an automobile provided for him… but has to buy his own tires, gasoline and supplies." This sounded as though he were speaking metaphorically, but it was true: The Vice President was given a car that he could use, but he was expected to operate and maintain it out of his own pocket (though the government did throw in a $1,000-a-month chauffeur).

He wasted no time making himself at home in the Senate, replacing the big chair used by his previous Vice Presidents because his feet couldn't touch the floor. After a sincere tribute from the Senate to its presiding officer, he wrote off his election to "an ignorant electorate." He also didn't help himself by suggesting, in effect, that the victims of the torpedoed *Lusitania* were asking for it.

Serving as regent on the board of the Smithsonian Institution as part of his official capacity as Vice President, Marshall jokingly asked if the Smithsonian had ever considered excavating the streets of the capital, since, given the primitive gait and demeanor of those currently walking the thoroughfares, prehistoric man was probably not buried far below. It was a telling moment for Marshall: "And then the utter uselessness and frivolity of the vice-presidency was disclosed, for not a man smiled. It was a year before I had courage to open my mouth again."

He accepted the city and his limitations—both his own and those of his job—and set down in writing a philosophy for his new gig: "To acknowledge the insignificant influence of the office; to take it in a good-natured way; to be friendly and well disposed to political friend and foe alike, to be loyal to my chief and at the same time not to be offensive to my associates." In other words, juſt know that you mean nothing, don't make waves, and you'll get your paycheck every Friday.

PLEASE DO NOT FEED THE VEEP

Marshall's firſt office was in the corridor behind the Senate chambers. Accuſtomed perhaps to the sleepier atmosphere of the Indiana ſtatehouse, he would often leave his office door open, only to hear Senate tour guides pointing out the Vice President to the surprised and curious mumblings of the tour groups. Finally, one day Marshall approached the open door and called out, "If you look on me as a wild animal, be kind enough to throw peanuts at me."

Fun Facts

Marshall's only real claim to fame is the phrase, "What this country needs is a good five-cent cigar." In faĉt, that line originated in the Kin Hubbard comic ſtrip *Abe Martin of Brown County*. Marshall saw it in the ſtrip and repeated it on the floor of the Senate, and it was forever after ascribed to him.

Marshall was the firſt Vice President since John C. Calhoun to win re-eleĉtion.

...AND ALL I GOT WAS THIS LOUSY STROKE

President Wilson devoted the last half of his second term to securing the U.S. entry into the League of Nations. When Republicans like Henry Cabot Lodge threatened to stall or kill U.S. ratification of the Treaty of Versailles—which included the League of Nations charter—Wilson took to the rails to rally public support, even saying that he would give his life for the cause of the League. God was apparently willing to greenlight that deal, but bad faith and poor follow-through on both sides effectively scuttled it. In Colorado, Wilson had a massive, permanently debilitating stroke. It wasn't enough to kill him, which probably would have garnered enough sympathy to get the Treaty ratified, but it all but ended his ability to govern. Had Marshall been allowed to step in as President, the goodwill alone might have been sufficient to move the Treaty through the Senate. Instead, the President's wife, doctors, and tight circle of advisers closed ranks and set up an obscuring window dressing around the Presidency. The President was fine and on the road to recovery!

In reality, the Vice President and virtually the entire U.S. government were kept out of the loop and held hostage by "a petticoat government" as one Senator put it: the President's wife kept visitors away, and decided which articles of business should be brought before the President. It was even whispered that it was her hand that put his signature on important documents, helping keep the severity of his illness a secret and keeping him in the Presidency. Even when Mrs. Wilson suggested it might be best to hand the reigns over to Marshall, it was Wilson's doctor who intervened, saying it would be bad for the President and for the world if the President entrusted to anyone else his shepherding of the Treaty through the Senate.

Meanwhile, they did little but arouse suspicion and distrust among Congress and the citizenry. To the bitter end Wilson refused to compromise, and the Treaty went down to defeat in the Senate. The U.S. never joined the League of Nations, and historians are left to wonder what would have happened to America, Europe, the world, and the legacy of Tom Marshall had he been allowed to take the wheel and navigate his own way through the Treaty debate.

CALVIN COOLIDGE
REPUBLICAN, MASSACHUSETTS
WITH WARREN G. HARDING, 1921–23

For the God-fearing, the teetotalers, the temperance advocates, and the like, Warren Harding was a nightmare. Certainly he was almoſt no one's firſt choice at the 1920 Republican convention. Said one delegate of Harding's nomination, "If you nominate Harding… you will bring shame to the country."

Harding and his running mate, the somnolent, teetotaling Calvin Coolidge, won the nomination and eleċtion. During his brief tenure as President, Harding kept the White House awash in whiskey, gambling, corruption, and adultery. He would die on a trip to the Weſt Coaſt in 1923, shortly after receiving an apparently diſturbing message detailing new inſtances of corruption uncovered in his Adminiſtration.

Benign, sober, dishrag-boring—Calvin "Silent Cal" Coolidge was for many the perfeċt antidote to the besotted, philandering, criminally associated Harding, who has come to be ranked as one of the worſt Presidents ever.

"AND THE MYSTERIOUS DELEGATE FROM OREGON, SOON TO BE LOST FOREVER TO HISTORY, WISHES TO NOMINATE…"

After Harding won on the tenth ballot, the final order of business was to nominate a Vice Presidential candidate, and it had already been decided that it was to be Senator Irvine Lenroot of Wisconsin. As Senator Medill McCormack of Illinois was reading Lenroot's nominating speech, from among the Oregon delegation came a cry of "Coolidge!" McCormick attempted to continue, but once again, "Coolidge!," and then again, and again. McCormick completed his speech, and the nomination was seconded and appeared to be heading for a vote. The man from Oregon demanded the floor. Convention Chairman Henry Cabot Lodge had given the dais over to an aċting chairman who, inſtead of ruling the man from Oregon out of order, gave him the floor to speak his piece. The man, Mr. Wallace McClamant, ſtood upon his chair and began a speech that was praċtically inaudible, but enough people apparently heard his laſt words— "… for the exalted office of Vice President Governor Calvin Coolidge, of Massachusetts"—because Coolidge beſted Lenroot, 674.5 to 146.

*"Mr. Coolidge's genius for inactivity is developed to
a very high point. It is not an indolent inactivity.
It is a grim, determined, alert inactivity, which keeps
Mr. Coolidge occupied constantly."*
—Columnist Walter Lippmann, 1926

It's said that McClamant had read Coolidge's book, *Have Faith In Massachusetts*, and was very taken with the governor. Another grand accident of history: If not for one oddly passionate man from Oregon, we all would have grown up studying the legacy of President Lenroot.

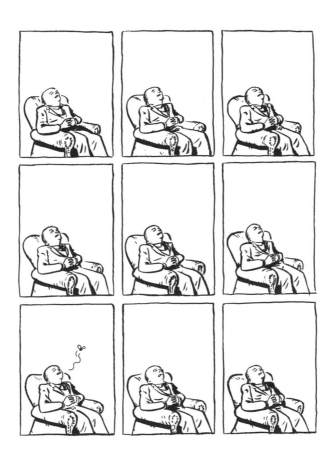

BY THE POWER VESTED IN ME FOR RAISING YOU, YOU LITTLE BASTARD

Cal was visiting his father when he received news that President Harding had died on a train to Alaska, and that he, Coolidge, was to become President. He quickly dispatched his father to issue the oath of office.

Colonel John Coolidge was tickled at the honor, swearing his son in as the 30th President of the United States. Cal went back to bed, while his father giddily sat up all night in his Sunday best. No one dared spoil the memory for him, but it was unclear whether or not a Massachusetts notary public could legally administer the oath of office to an incoming President of the United States, so a D.C. Supreme Court judge later re-administered the oath just to be on the safe side.

COOLIDGESE

It was said of Coolidge that when he opened his mouth, a moth flew out. He was far more taciturn than one would expect of a politician, much less a President or Vice President. But he used his silence and economy of speech to dish out humor a great deal sharper than most historians give him credit for. Coolidge, Will Rogers once said, "wasted more humor on folks than almost anybody."

Fun Facts

As presiding officer of the Senate, Coolidge would eat lunch alone at a corner table in the Senate dining room, facing the wall.

Coolidge slept 10-11 hours a day, with a nap in the afternoon.

Coolidge was the first President to appear in a sound movie, the Lee DeForest film *President Coolidge, Taken On The White House Lawn.*

Among his pearls of wit during his tenure in the White House:

"You lose."
— The notoriously reserved Silent Cal to a dinner hostess,
who bet that she could get him to say more than two words.

"Well, don't you think they ought to be represented, too?"
— Coolidge, debating the selection of Cabinet members to an adviser,
who dismissed a certain industrialist under consideration as "a son of
a bitch."

"Goodbye. I have had a very enjoyable time in Washington."
— Coolidge's 1929 Presidential farewell.

"I had a grandmother. She was a Baptist. She didn't."
— Coolidge, being asked at a dinner party to join a conversation on
whether it was acceptable to play golf on Sunday.

POLE NUMBERS

Illinois Congresswoman Ruth Hanna McCormick wanted
Coolidge to appoint a Polish Chicagoan from her district to the federal bench. To Coolidge's annoyance, she was relentless in lobbying him
for the appointment, and finally brought along a delegation of Polish
Americans to help make her case. In Coolidge's office, he said nothing to the group gathered before him and merely stared at the floor
for a very long, very uncomfortable period of time. Finally, he noted,
"Mighty fine carpet there," with no enthusiasm and little inflection.

Representative McCormick's delegation nervously smiled and
agreed.

"New one," said Coolidge. "Cost a lot of money."

More awkward silence. Finally he gestured at McCormick and
said to the Polish-American delegation, "She wore out the old one
trying to get you a judge." And that was the end of their visit.

 # CHARLES GATES DAWES
REPUBLICAN, ILLINOIS
WITH CALVIN COOLIDGE, 1925–29

More Vice Presidents than not have taken the oath as bland nonentities, who by their prosaic nature haven't concerned themselves with landing a meaningful place in the pantheon of America's seconds-in-charge. Instead, they went about their undemanding, unappreciated, and occasionally demeaning jobs, free if they chose to perpetuate their own mediocrity and maybe even sully their reputations from time to time.

Not so for America's 30th VP, Charles Dawes. With the esteem and dignity of a Nobel Prize to his credit (for his plan to help Germany deal with reparations after World War I), he faced a challenge that few of his predecessors or successors would: He would have to go that extra mile to besmirch his name, lest he pass into history as one of the most sensible, even-keeled, and uncontroversial men ever to hold the office. Thanks to a few well-executed incidents, he did not go unblemished into that good night.

*"Barkley, this is a hell of a job. I can only do two things: one is to
sit up here and listen to you birds talk…The other is to look at the
newspapers every morning to see how the President's health is."*
—Vice President Dawes, chatting with
Senator Alben Barkley.

"HUMBLED AND HONORED, I STAND BEFORE YOU CALLOW, PERNICIOUS SCOUNDRELS…"

Coolidge was already less than pleased with his Vice President-elect for presumptuously informing the President that, if he invited Dawes to attend Cabinet meetings, it would set a bad precedent and he would have to refuse on principle. Coolidge had never indicated he would extend such an invitation, but that didn't stop Dawes from preemptively opining on the subject, or from sending a copy of the letter to the press and embarrassing his boss.

He had a bigger audacity planned for Inauguration Day, though. Standing for the first time before the Senate over which he was to preside, Dawes opened up on the stunned body with a scolding, finger-wagging, 20-minute speech lambasting them on matters of protocol and calling for the abolition of the filibuster rule, daring any of the Senators to oppose him. The "icy silence" that reportedly greeted Dawes after his speech soon gave way to far more animated reprisals from many of the 96 Senators from both sides of the aisle, who—thanks to Dawes—were kicking off the new Congress in a rare display of unity. "Brutal and clownish" was how Senator Walter George described the new Vice President's get-to-know-ya address. Other comments included, "Exactly what should not have been said," "a spectacle," and "an occasion…perverted into a farce."

Even worse, he managed to completely upstage the normally unexcitable Cal, who had looked forward to his inauguration as the pinnacle of his long career in public service. Sitting in the audience with steam coming off his ears, Coolidge likely wished the convention had picked Hoover for his running mate instead.

STUPID IS AS STUPID DAWES

It wasn't long before Dawes learned how ill-advised his first-day-on-the-job tirade had been. Senate Democrats would very soon offer this parliamentary neophyte a lesson on who really held the power in Washington. On what was sure to be a close confirmation vote for Coolidge's choice for Attorney General, Charles Warren of Michigan, Cal was counting on his Vice President to gather the necessary votes and be there to cast the tiebreaker if necessary. Checking the roster of scheduled Democratic speakers and conferring with the Republican leadership, Dawes was confident that the vote would not take place until later in the day, and repaired to the Willard Hotel for his customary siesta.

The Dems were well aware of Dawes' afternoon repose and kicked their plan into action, suspending their planned speeches one by one and moving the issue towards a vote. Panicked Republicans sent word to the Willard Hotel to tell the Vice President what was happening and urge that he make all possible haste for the Capitol, as it looked like he may need to cast the tiebreaker. His frantic dash was too late—

Fun Facts

In 1911, amateur pianist and flautist Charles Dawes wrote the music for what would become Tommy Edwards' 1951 #1 pop hit, "It's All In The Game."

Dawes was the great-great-grandson of William Dawes, who accompanied Paul Revere on his "The British are coming!" midnight ride.

Dawes earned the nickname "Hell'n Maria" during a House of Representatives hearing on World War I military expenditures as chief of supply procurement for the American Expeditionary Force. Responding to a question to which he pounded his fist and shouted, "Hell and Maria! We weren't trying to keep a set of books over there, we were trying to win a war!"

and unnecessary as it turned out—because one Democratic Senator changed his vote in support of Warren to a vote against. Dawes was the laughingstock of Washington for a time, and the President, embarrassed at the spectacle and already fed up with Dawes, had little use for his Vice President from that point forward. One snarky observer posted a sign outside the Willard: "Dawes Slept Here."

CHARLES CURTIS
REPUBLICAN, KANSAS
WITH HERBERT HOOVER, 1929–33

C alvin Coolidge bowed out of the Presidency in typically terse Coolidge style, passing a note to reporters in South Dakota's Black Hills where he was vacationing: "I do not choose to run for President in 1928."

Suddenly the jostling was on among potential successors. Vice President Dawes did not immediately commit to being a candidate, but other short-listers included Senator Charles Curtis and the Vice Presidential finalists from 1924—Governor Lowden of Idaho (who had refused the nomination) and Secretary of Commerce Herbert Hoover (whom the convention refused). Emerging from the pack was Hoover, who had never run for elective office and about whom the outgoing President said, "That man has offered me unsolicited advice for six years—all of it bad!"

With that ringing endorsement, the Republicans chose Hoover on the first ballot, and he quickly offered the nation some insight into why Coolidge had reason to suspect Hoover's counsel and analytical acumen. In his acceptance speech, he proudly declared, "We in America today are nearer to the final triumph over poverty than ever before in the history of any land." That was exciting news to an America on the eve of the booming, wildly prosperous 1930s.

The delegates were just as shrewd in their judgment, selecting as Hoover's number two the 68-year-old Senator Curtis of Kansas, who was dismissed by writer Oswald Garrison Villard as "the apotheosis of mediocrity," and who had said about the man with whom he would be running, "Why should we nominate a man for whom we will have to apologize throughout the campaign?"

With such a positive, united, and forward-thinking ticket, it's no surprise that the American voters elected Hoover and Curtis in a landslide. Happy days were here again!

INDIAN LIVER

Curtis was very proud of his Native American heritage, having grown up on a reservation and learning to ride bareback as a boy. He was conspicuous and relentless in using his Native American lineage for political gain, so much so that it was impossible to separate

"Charles Curtis of Kansas, one-eighth Kaw,
and seven-eighths incompetent."
—Vice Presidential historian Sol Barzman,
playing on the fact that Curtis referred to himself as being
"one-eighth Kaw and 100% Republican."

Curtis the politician from Curtis the Kaw Indian. H.L. Mencken would refer to the President and his VP as "Lord Hoover and the Injun." During Curtis' House days, Speaker Tom Reed became rather fond of "the Indian," and on one occasion—when Curtis thought he'd interrupted the Speaker and excused himself—Reed called after him, "Come back in here, Indian, I want you to hear this!"

During the '28 campaign, he made liberal use of the declaration "from Kaw teepee to the Capitol" and would pose for pictures in exotic headdresses and festoon his office in American Indian artifacts.

THAT'S MR. VICE PRESIDENT TO YOU, COMMONER

The closer Curtis got to the White House, the more arrogant and insufferable he became (as one writer reported, "his humility turned inside out"). While he was a Senator he was affable and easygoing, known as "Charley" by his colleagues. Shortly after he was elected Vice President, however, an old colleague came up to congratulate his friend in the familiar way he'd come to address him. The erstwhile "Charley" was none too happy. "Where do you get that 'Charley' stuff? Don't you know I am Vice President now?"

SISTER ACT

Curtis' wife died five years before he took office, and into her shoes stepped his sister, Dolly Gann. To the horror of proper establishment Washington, Curtis insisted she assume what would have been his wife's place at state dinners and other high-profile soirées. This was offensive to polite D.C. society and the popular wags of the day not just because of its creepy incestuous overtones, but because Dolly's very-much-living husband was relegated to ghostly obscurity. After yet another dinner where Dolly attended at her brother's arm, Nebraska Senator George Norris remarked sarcastically of Dolly's supplanted spouse, "I had the impression all along that Mrs. Gann would get what she wanted. Mr. Gann, however, is left wholly unprovided for—which is exactly as I feared. I refuse to abandon him in this crisis. I do not intend to let this matter rest until I am assured that he will at least have a snack wherever he goes."

DEPRESSION? NO, EVERYONE'S JUST A LITTLE BLUE

Not everyone was depressed by the collapse of the mighty American economy. Charles' sister didn't so much ignore the newly starving elephant in the room, as she was completely oblivious of it. Living the lavish life of a Vice President's… sister, Dolly figured this Depression everyone spoke of was much ado about nothing. In a feel-good speech she gave on behalf of the Hoover Administration, while many Ameri-

Fun Facts

Curtis was the last U.S. President or Vice President to wear facial hair.

The 1932 George & Ira Gershwin musical *Of Thee I Sing* featured a Vice President named Alexander Throttlebottom, who was clearly modeled after Curtis. VP Throttlebottom could only get into the White House on public tours, and "last week, he tried to join the library, but he needed two references, so he couldn't get in."

cans were adjusting to their new lifestyles of ever-present hunger, chronic unemployment, and abject poverty, she cheerfully declared that the Depression was over and everything was fine, prompting a newspaper to sarcastically trumpet in a headline the next day, "Dolly Calls It Off."

YOU DAMNED DIRTY APES!

Proving himself something less than an empathetic man of the people, Charles was unmoved, appalled, and even afraid for his safety when a literal army of hungry, unemployed World War I veterans gathered outside his office demanding jobs and food. Curtis summoned the Marines to disperse the motley lot of them, which unfortunately escalated matters until President Hoover dispatched General Douglas MacArthur to bring his own troops and teargas to accomplish what Curtis' Marines could not.

The issue came up on the campaign trail in 1932 in Las Vegas, where someone asked Curtis why he didn't feed the former soldiers. "I've fed more than you have, you dirty cowards! I'm not afraid of any of you!" Hoover and Curtis would go on that November to lose Nevada—and 44 other States.

John Nance Garner
Democrat, Texas
With Franklin Delano Roosevelt, 1933–41

The Vice Presidency has spelled the dismal and often undignified end to a not-insignificant number of political careers. Many of those careers, though, have belonged to middling gray suits and men of uninspiring character who, had they lived today, would probably have gone to their twilight years on a quietly desperate path paved with middling corporate board appointments and an occasional mention in their hometown paper when they showed up to present a tiara to the 4th of July Princess or cut the opening ribbon at the Nalley's plant. Faced with that definition of mediocrity, joining a winning Presidential ticket was a no-lose proposition and practically a dream come true. Only one, though, would cast aside a job he'd spent his whole life striving towards (and in fact had only recently attained) and sacrifice perhaps two decades of political viability and job security to serve in the nation's number two elected office. Here, John Nance Garner stands alone.

Born in a log cabin during the Grant Presidency, Garner pulled himself up from nothing to become a lawyer, judge, and 14-term U.S. Representative from a very safe Texas district, finally realizing his dream of becoming Speaker of the House in 1931. He could have left well enough alone and remained, if not Speaker, at least in his seat for another twenty or thirty years. But, like so many who find out what it's like to fly so high, he thought he could go higher and went after the Presidency in 1932. After losing the Democratic nomination to Franklin Delano Roosevelt, he could have taken his comfortable seat along with the rest of the 73rd Congress, but he was offered the second spot and accepted it, thinking he could still be President, even if it meant having to serve nearly a decade under FDR. "I gave up the second most important job in Government for eight long years as Roosevelt's spare tire," he would say. "Worst damn fool mistake I ever made."

"THE CHAIR RECOGNIZES THE CLUMSY LITTLE MAN FROM ITALY"

Garner was inches from being inaugurated not as Vice President, but President. On February 15, 1933, President-elect Roosevelt was in Miami, shaking hands with Chicago Mayor Anton Cermak,

"(It's) not worth a bucket of warm piss."
—John Nance Garner sharing his opinion of
the Vice Presidency with fellow Texan Lyndon Johnson.

when Giuseppe Zangara, a young immigrant literally driven crazy by excruciating pain in his gall bladder, attempted to assassinate FDR from just 25 feet away. Being only five feet tall, he couldn't see his target over the crowds and had to stand on an unsteady folding chair, which went wobbly under his legs. His shots missed the incoming President, killing Cermak instead. Nothing against Garner really, but he was no FDR. Said historian Alan Brinkley, "The New Deal, the move toward internationalism—these would never have happened. It would have changed the history of the world in the 20th century. I don't think the Kennedy assassination changed things as much as Roosevelt's would have."

THREE-TERM LOSER

For just over a term, Roosevelt and Garner were an able enough team, with Garner working with Congress to help push through much of FDR's New Deal legislation. By the end of their second term, though, FDR's advisers were referring to Garner as "that political billy goat from Texas," while Garner was coming to despise FDR for a number of governance oversteps (attempting to pack the Supreme Court with justices who would be friendlier to his proposals, for example), as well as for breaking a sacrosanct American tradition and aiming for a third term (Garner was old enough to remember the rancorous comments in his own home when Grant considered a third term). There was no way he would be on board for a third term as FDR's VP, and, if he had his way, FDR wouldn't be serving a third term at all. As sitting Vice President, he announced he would be challenging his President in 1940.

Garner had made some missteps of his own and already had a few strikes against him. He'd enraged the labor bloc by opposing changes in the Wages-Hours Act, and poked liberal and black voters in the eye by refusing to endorse a concert by black contralto Marian Anderson at the Lincoln Memorial (Anderson had already been denied the use of Constitution Hall by the Daughters of the American Revolution, as well as the auditorium of a local white high school by the D.C. Board of Education). In the run for the nomination, Garner was crushed, and FDR cruised to a third term with a new running mate, Henry Agard Wallace. Garner was still in good health, and—had he remained in the House instead of accepting the Vice Presidency—he likely could have served many more years in Washington. Instead, embittered by the events in his last few years as Vice President, he retired to Texas, where he lived another 27 years.

Fun Facts

On his 95th birthday, Garner received a happy birthday call from John F. Kennedy, who was visiting Texas. Said Garner, "You're my President and I love you. I hope you stay in there forever." Kennedy would stay in there just a few more hours. This was November 22, 1963.

Dying just over two weeks shy of his 99th birthday, Garner lived longer than any President or Vice President in history.

HENRY AGARD WALLACE
DEMOCRAT, IOWA
WITH FRANKLIN DELANO ROOSEVELT, 1941–45

I f FDR had died just a few months earlier, the postwar world would have gone in a much different direction. Henry Agard Wallace, though fundamentally decent, highly intelligent, and widely respected by the electorate, was a man whose intellectual curiosity led him down roads best left untraveled by a Chief Executive. He was no Harry Truman and, by nearly every objective political standard, the most oddly calibrated bird ever to sit a heartbeat away from the Presidency.

SIS BOOM... WHA?

Wallace's formative matriculation was a few galaxies removed from that of his would-be political contemporaries. Instead of pledging a fraternity, preparing for law school, and sporting a raccoon overcoat and "Go State!" pennant, Wallace's undergraduate years were spent studying Animal Husbandry. In a move that surely would have prepared him to hold his own at Yalta, he later changed his field of study to Corn Genetics. He carried this interest into his political life, augmenting it with a religious curiosity that led him to explore Catholicism, Judaism, Buddhism, Humanistic Darwinism, Muhammadanism, Zoroastrianism, and Christian Science. It was with this educational and avocational resume that he ascended to the Vice Presidency of the United States. A writer would say of Wallace that he "gives me an eerie feeling that he isn't really listening to me..." and that he seemed to consider himself "a man of destiny, a person answering the calls the rest of us don't hear."

PORTRAITS BY THE MESSIAH AS A YOUNG MAN

One of the mystical personas Wallace was attracted to was a man named Nicholas Konstantinovich Roerich, who was a 1929 Nobel Prize winner, as well as the charter—and only—member of something called the "Great White Brotherhood." He filled Wallace's head with fanciful tales of a young Jesus Christ having visited Tibet and left behind thousands of his own paintings. Wallace, acting in his capacity as Secretary of Agriculture, sent Roerich on official USDA business

> *"When I die, I would like to have one thing on my headstone: that I was the man who kept Henry Wallace from becoming President of the United States."*
> — Democratic National Committee chairman Robert Hannegan, on replacing Wallace with Harry S Truman on the '44 Democratic ticket.

to Mongolia to search for drought-resistant grasses, though rumors flew that Wallace was using his government imprimatur and taxpayer dollars to authorize Roerich to search for everything from the lost Jesus paintings to a Buddhist utopia to the second coming of Christ. (Roerich's trip was eventful, but in a much less mystical way: he was arrested by the Chinese on suspicion of spying, and, in his absence from the U.S., was charged there with tax evasion.)

That was the end of Wallace's association with Roerich, until some of Roerich's "Dear Guru" letters from Wallace surfaced. These included crypto-New Age/Masonic rhetorical flourishes like "I have been thinking of holding the casket—the sacred, most precious casket. And I have thought of the New Country going forth to meet the seven stars under the sign of the three stars. And I have thought of the admonition 'Await the Stone.' We await the Stone and we welcome you again to this glorious land of destiny."

This is about as far as you can get from shooting someone in the face, but both are approximately equal as barometers of Vice Presidential fitness. But give Wallace some credit: Certainly Dan Quayle's archivists have never found in his papers anything close to such mellifluous, otherworldly musings, much less anything that didn't express the word "destiny" as "density."

HOGOCAUST

As Secretary of Agriculture, Wallace encouraged farmers to plow under some 10 million acres of cotton and take the machete to 6 million pigs in an effort to bolster the market and improve prices. The plan worked, but the *Chicago Tribune* lambasted Wallace as "the biggest butcher in Christendom." Unmoved, Wallace said of his critics, "Perhaps they think that farmers should run a sort of old-folks home for hogs."

"THE KLINGON DELEGATION SECONDS THE NOMINATION"

To say that FDR's selection of Wallace unnerved the delegates would be an understatement. A pantheistic, utopian, hybridist Agriculture Secretary who audited Presbyterian sermons and Roman Catholic masses for fun didn't seem like a draw for any significant number of on-the-fence voters. Yet, despite the boos and catcalls at the convention, Roosevelt was adamant, and Wallace won the nomination in a close vote over House Speaker William Bankhead of Alabama. The mood in the convention hall was so foul that Wallace eschewed the traditional acceptance speech.

Wallace was a polarizing and impolitic Vice President. He didn't fit in well with the "boys club" of the Senate, and didn't get off to a good start when he shut down the infamous "board of education," a makeshift bar where his predecessor would invite Congressmen for afternoons of cocktails and cigars. His undoing was an ugly, protracted, and public feud with Secretary of Commerce Jesse Jones over the allocation of wartime supplies. Roosevelt dumped Wallace from the ticket in '44, to the deafeningly audible relief of much of his party.

Fun Facts

After leaving politics, Wallace devoted his energies to developing hybrid seed and a new breed of leghorn chicken that produced more eggs than conventional chickens. It would become for a time the most popular egg-laying fowl in the world.

Wallace disliked the Senators as much as they disliked him. In a friendly boxing match with Senator Allan Ellender of Louisiana, Wallace KO'd his critic and adversary.

His successor, Harry S Truman, assumed the Presidency just 82 days after Wallace left office.

"I LOVE WHAT YOU'VE DONE WITH THE PLACE!"

In 1944, FDR sent Wallace on a tour of Asia. In Siberia, his Soviet hosts squired him about in style and took him to a bustling gold-mining center called Magadan. Wallace, an ardent admirer of Stalin's Soviet Union and a proponent of a one-world government, was dazzled, describing it as a productive hive of human enterprise, "a combination TVA and Hudson's Bay Company." Unfortunately, Magadan was actually a slave labor camp the Soviets had slapped a figurative coat of paint on, Potemkin village-style, in anticipation of Wallace's visit.

Nearly a decade later, Wallace would publish his mea culpa, *Where I Was Wrong*, writing that he was a bit too quick and naïve to give Stalin the benefit of the doubt.

HARRY S TRUMAN
DEMOCRAT, MISSOURI
WITH FRANKLIN DELANO ROOSEVELT, 1945

George W. Bush has said that he believes that his beleaguered, bloodied reputation will one day undergo rehabilitation on the level of the once-reviled Harry S Truman. One can't predict the future, of course, but some significant differences between the two men already exist. First, the voracious Truman would go to bed every night with his green eyeshade on while reading expansive historical tomes covering such weighty figures as Nebuchadnezzar and Cyrus the Great. One shouldn't presume to know what George Bush reads when he goes to bed, but it's probably a fairly safe bet that he wouldn't get past the front cover of a Nebuchadnezzar biography.

The second difference is that Bush was never Vice President. But for a few months and, many would say, the intervention of a merciful God, Harry Truman very nearly wasn't either. As the 1944 election approached, it was not a well-kept secret that the ailing President was circling the drain. When the scramble to select his running mate kicked off, most were well aware that they would likely be selecting only a temporary Vice President. There were many God-fearing Democrats who were terrified that the seemingly deranged, Utopian, Red-hugging Henry Wallace would fall arse-backwards into the job, and then there wouldn't be a deity in the Universe that could or would save us from Hitler and Stalin ruling our once-proud, shamelessly capitulated United States.

As writer George Allen more pithily noted, the Roosevelt brain trust consisting of national Democratic Party Chairman Robert Hannegan, Party Treasurer Edwin Pauley, New York Democratic party head Edward J. Flynn, and Postmaster General Frank Walker "were determined that Roosevelt's successor would not be the boomerang-throwing mystic from the place where the tall corn grows."

That was the order of the day leading up to the 1944 convention. The powerbrokers considered Senate Majority Leader Alben Barkley, Supreme Court Justice William O. Douglas, Senator Jimmy Byrnes, Indiana Senator Sherman Minton, House Speaker Sam Rayburn, and Missouri Senator Harry S Truman.

For his loyalty and proximity to the President—and the fact that he really wanted the job—Jimmy Byrnes was the obvious choice. He'd

"Look at all the Vice Presidents in history. Where are they?
They were about as useful as a cow's fifth teat."
—Harry S Truman, to *Time* magazine, January 18, 1954,
explaining why he never wanted to be Vice President.

earned the appellation "Assistant President" and was said by many to be
Roosevelt's first preference. But he was a Southern Boy whose presence
on the ticket, it was believed, would hurt the black vote. Worse, in the
eyes of labor, he was a wolf in wolves' clothing. Labor was putting its
full support behind Wallace, though they could have been persuaded to
back a second candidate on the Vice Presidential short list—one Harry
S Truman. Truman told labor leaders not to give it a second thought,
because he wasn't a candidate.

The only opinion that seemingly mattered, though, was that of the
President, and he had indicated at a number of junctures that Byrnes
was his boy. (Like a popular girl at the prom too flattered to turn down
any of her suitors, FDR supported everyone—Truman, Douglas, Byrnes,
and his "old friend" Wallace—and would publicly reject no one. Instead,
he left that ugly business to the four party operatives and the Convention.) As it stood, then, going into the 1944 Democratic Convention at
Chicago, Byrnes thought he had the President's full support and had
even enlisted as his nominator none other than one Harry S Truman.

Despite his often vehement insistence that he was not a candidate
for the second spot on the ticket—and despite a Gallup Poll giving Truman less than 2% support on a list of candidates for the nomination—it
seems in retrospect that the choice of Harry S Truman to become the
34th Vice President of the United States was preordained by the party
elders who didn't want Wallace and were having trouble finding a viable
candidate who would both accept the nomination and be acceptable to
Roosevelt.

Truman, though, was really just another accident of history, and,
many would argue, the most fortuitous accident to grace world democracy in the 20th century. Neither the Vice Presidency nor the Presidency
were ever part of Harry Truman's planned career trajectory. Truman
came very late in life to politics. After a stint in banking, he spent the

years leading up to World War I working on a 600-acre farm juſt south of Kansas City. He was on the far side of his 30s when he served as an infantryman in the War. Back in Missouri after the Armiſtice, he and a friend, Edward Jacobsen, ran a haberdashery, which soon fell viĉtim to the poſt-war recession. With his 40s in sight, and with the help of ſtoried Kansas City machine boss Tom Prendergaſt, Truman assumed his firſt political position as Jackson County Commissioner. After losing one eleĉtion, Truman returned for two terms as the county's chief executive officer, predominately presiding over the conſtruĉtion and maintenance of county roads. In 1934, Truman was Prendergaſt's candidate for the Democratic nomination for U.S. Senator, winning the nomination and eventually crushing Republican incumbent Roscoe Patterson in the general eleĉtion.

Truman won re-eleĉtion in 1940 despite a bruising primary fight againſt Roosevelt's secret favorite, Missouri Governor Lloyd C. Stark, and Federal Attorney Maurice Milligan, who had made his bones working towards the deſtruĉtion of the notorious Prendergaſt Machine, incarcerating its namesake, not to mention the brother of one of Truman's 1934 primary opponents, Tuck Milligan.

It was in his second senatorial term where Truman made his name and percolated to the top of the pot that would be skimmed for 1944's Vice Presidential candidates. He headed the Truman Commission (or, in bloated governmental parlance, "the Senate Special Committee to Inveſtigate the National Defense Program") and traveled tirelessly across the country inveſtigating fraud and waſte within the national defense apparatus. His efforts saved the government a whopping $15 billion (nearly $222 billion in 2007 dollars).

"I'M SORRY, THAT WAS A 'NAY' AND NOT A 'NO' THAT WE NEEDED. THE 'AYES' HAVE IT"

In a praĉtice probably not endorsed by Robert's Rules of Order, the powerbrokers at the 1944 eleĉtion were quaking in their kingmaking boots at the prospeĉt of a Wallace Vice Presidential re-nomination by acclamation, and took draſtic aĉtion when the firſt roll call votes showed Wallace trouncing the Senator from Missouri. This simply would not ßtand, and they were fortunate enough to be holding the convention in Chicago, a city notoriously friendly to Democratic interests. The city's mayor, Ed Kelly, was accommodating enough to declare the hall in violation of city fire code, and, ordering it cleared immediately, gave the de facto steering committee time to twist some arms and turn the tide away from the pro-Wallace vote. Only a handful answered Chairman Samuel D. Jackson's motion with "ayes," but there was a widespread grumbling of "No! No!" among Wallace supporters. Pretending to not hear any "Nays," Jackson (who clearly did not want to see a Wallace nomination) carried the motion.

What a difference a good night's sleep makes—the first vote the next day saw a widespread change of heart, and Wallace's lead scalped to an insufficient majority of 429.5 to 319.5 for Truman (589 was needed for nomination). By the second ballot, the delegates were a little clearer on what was expected of them, and registered 477.5 for Truman compared to 473 for Wallace. By the time a "revised" second ballot was logged, everyone was on the same page, and Truman shellacked the sitting Vice President by a final tally of 1031 to 105.

PAYING THE COST TO PLEASE THE BOSS

The Prendergast connection was a source of continued irritation for Truman. Though he never took money or fulfilled any untoward quid pro quo for Prendergast ("He's the contrariest man on earth," Tom Prendergast once complained), his mere association with the man who would eventually go to prison for tax evasion related to his long career in graft and municipal corruption was a cudgel Truman's opponents often tried to use on him, albeit with little success.

Truman's connection to Prendergast and his fabled machine was accidental but classically parochial: Harry had served in World War I with Jim Prendergast, who was the son of Tom Prendergast's brother, Mike, who helped control local operations.

Tom Prendergast died a broken man in January 1945, and the Vice President-elect raised eyebrows, hackles, and worse when he chose to return to Missouri to attend his old patron's funeral. It was utterly inappropriate for an incoming Vice President to pay respects to a felon as notorious as Prendergast. Always his own man, Truman said, "Bosh!" with a wave of his hand and went to the funeral anyway. He said of his former patron, "He was always my friend and I have always been his."

CRITICAL ASS

Washington Post music critic Paul Hume dared to write an honest, if somewhat brutal, review of First Daughter Margaret Truman's singing recital in 1950: "... Miss Truman cannot sing very well. She is flat a good deal of the time—more so last night than at any time we have heard her in past years." He hadn't reckoned with the man who rightly earned the nickname, "Give 'Em Hell Harry," but he soon received the full brunt of a father's rage when Truman, on his morning walk, dropped Hume a letter saying, among other salty and un-Presidential things, "You sound like a frustrated old man who never made a success, an eight-ulcer man on a four-ulcer job, with all four ulcers working. I never met you, but if I do you'll need a new nose and a supporter below."

The letter, of course, was made public, but the majority of letter writers to the *Post* supported Truman's position.

Fun Facts

The lack of a period after Harry S Truman's middle initial may or may not be an accident. The "S" was for his grandfathers, Anderson Shipp Truman and Solomon Young. Truman said in 1962 that it was a compromise, hence the fact that most historians wrote "S" rather than "S." He went on to recommend that reporters should omit the period. However, many of Truman's subsequent signatures and the recommendations of certain style guides suggest using the period. Jest or not—and since no one knows for sure—we'll stick with Mr. Truman's 1962 recommendation.

Never one to equivocate, Truman said in June 1941, "If we see that Germany is winning we ought to help Russia and if Russia is winning we ought to help Germany, and that way let them kill as many as possible, although I don't want to see Hitler victorious under any circumstances. Neither of them thinks anything of their pledged word."

ALBEN W. BARKLEY
DEMOCRAT, KENTUCKY
WITH HARRY S TRUMAN, 1949–53

The Vice Presidency was the next-to-last stop in a long political career for Alben Barkley. He had been available since 1928 and was taking one last shot at the office, hoping to fill in one more blank on an already-full resume. After all, he was 70 years old in 1948 when Harry Truman attempted to become President in his own right, and he already had a comfortable day job as Senate Minority Leader. Truman was being left for dead even by his own party and was having considerable difficulty filling the second spot on the ticket, until Barkley finally called and asked to be his running mate. He had nothing to lose, and there was even a chance that he might become President—every 70-year-old boy's dream.

"TRUMAN DEFEATS DAILY TRIBUNE!"

The campaign of 1948 was a moribund affair for the Democrats, who fully and reasonably expected their standard-bearer to be clubbed senseless by Republican sure-thing, Governor Thomas Dewey. The Democrats had lost the Congress in 1946, and Truman's approval ratings plummeted to the 30s. Supreme Court Justice William O. Douglas had refused the VP nomination for the Dems, saying he had no desire to be second man on a ticket that was sure to be beaten so badly.

Fun Facts

In 1948, at 70 years of age and in an era without jet travel, Alben Barkley hit the campaign trail in a small plane, traveling 3,500 miles a day for six weeks across 26 states, sometimes giving as many as 15 speeches a day.

The nickname "Veep" was coined by Alben Barkley's grandson, after Barkley complained that "the Vice President of the United States" was too long.

Barkley is often credited with coining the phrase "Give 'em hell, Harry!," allegedly from his keynote address.

"Why didn't you tell me you wanted to be Vice President?"
—Harry Truman, after receiving Barkley's telephone inquiry.

Practically the only highlight at the Democratic Convention that year was the walkout of the Southern delegates when Hubert Humphrey began beating the podium for civil rights. Many Democrats were arguing that the party should just sit out the election and keep their powder dry for '52. "We're just mild about Harry" banners hung throughout the hall.

Then up came septuagenarian Barkley, who gave a keynote address that he called a "ripsnorter," stirring the delegates to life. "When my speech was over, the hitherto apathetic delegates were on their hind legs and cheering," Barkley said.

Barkley joined the ticket, he and Truman hit the road, and less than four months later they stunned the world—and possibly even their families and themselves—by defeating Dewey and his running mate Earl Warren.

VEEPSHOW

After running unsuccessfully for President in 1952, Barkley accepted a $2,500-a-week gig on NBC for a Sunday night show called *Meet The Veep,* where he shared folksy anecdotes about Washington and the White House, and fielded softball questions from host Earl Godwin.

AS YOU WISH

Barkley was giving a speech at Washington and Lee University in 1956, talking about a life in politics and discussing the differences between the two parties. "I'm glad to sit on the back row, for I would rather be a servant in the House of the Lord than to sit in the seats of the mighty." With that, right there at the rostrum, he dropped dead of a heart attack.

RICHARD M. NIXON
REPUBLICAN, CALIFORNIA
WITH DWIGHT D. EISENHOWER, 1953–61

I t's hard to imagine that Richard Nixon—all jowls and beady-eyed suspicion—was ever a youthful man, but there was a time when Nixon could answer a want ad for someone "young, vigorous, ready to learn," and that was in 1952 when WWII hero and GOP standard-bearer Dwight Eisenhower was looking for a running mate. In Nixon, he got a conservative young turk who could bridge the gap between two generations of Republicans, as well as an ardent anti-Communist, designated party attack dog, and left-coast native who could help deliver California's 32 electoral votes.

Nixon got a chance to take the next step in a meteoric rise to the top of a party that still looked askance at him. He had never been a warm and gregarious glad-hander, and his previous six years in politics did nothing to change that. He was as cold, stony, and eyes-on-his-books as he'd been throughout his ascetic Quaker upbringing.

Now, after nearly 20 years of Democratic rule, the Republicans had the chance to take back the White House. They had their first choice in Dwight Eisenhower, and his choice of running mate was the 39-year-old junior Senator from California, whose first trip to the Executive Branch would begin a chapter in American politics that's still reverberating today. And but for an adorable, wet-nosed little puppy, it was a long, wrenching, and scandalous chapter that very nearly didn't happen at all.

CHECKERED PASS

The 1952 election erupted in scandal in September with a *New York Post* headline decrying a "SECRET NIXON FUND." Not a money pile of Watergate proportions by any stretch, it amounted to $18,250 in contributions by fellow Republicans that Nixon claimed were expense reimbursements. An independent audit confirmed that there was nothing to the stink, but the Democrats were salivating at the opportunity to take out Eisenhower's tough, young lieutenant (even though there was a more unseemly stench rising from a larger pile of cash in Democratic nominee Adlai Stevenson's corner). The pro-Republican *New York Herald* and some close to Eisenhower began calling for Nixon to resign from the ticket. When Nixon heard

"Richard Nixon is a no good, lying bastard. If he ever caught himself telling the truth, he'd lie just to keep his hand in."
—Harry S Truman

that the Herald had opined that he should go, he suspected that this was Eisenhower's preference as well. It didn't help when Eisenhower, speaking with reporters, wondered aloud why they should run the campaign "if we ourselves aren't as clean as hound's tooth," or that mail and counsel coming into the campaign suggested an even split over whether Nixon should stay or go.

Nixon very nearly stepped down, but his friend Harold Stassen urged him to stay on. Nixon wanted the exonerating blessing that Eisenhower had seemed to offer when the scandal first broke, but Eisenhower wasn't about to commit himself, prompting Nixon to exhort, "General, there comes a time in matters like this when you need to either shit or get off the pot!"

Ike wasn't moved, and Nixon's pleas continued. The Republican party ponied up $75,000 to pay for a television appearance that allowed Nixon to explain the fairly legitimate, innocuous $18,000, since there was a feeling within the GOP that Ike couldn't win without him (After Truman's Lazarus rise in 1948, the party was more than a little skittish when anyone crowed about poll numbers).

Nixon turned in a masterful performance, and almost single-handedly gave birth to the modern media *mea culpa* (though in this instance there really was nothing for which to take the blame). He looked dolefully at the camera, and in minute detail defended the probity of his personal and campaign finances. He trotted out a line he'd used when he'd been heckled at a Eugene, Oregon campaign appearance a few days earlier, saying his wife Pat didn't wear a mink coat, but "a respectable Republican cloth coat."

The sap virtually gushed when he went in for his mawkish climax, defiantly claiming that the one gift he did accept which may have been inappropriate was "a little cocker spaniel dog… black and white, spotted, and our little girl, Tricia, named it Checkers. And you know, the kids… loved the dog, and I just want to say this, right now, that regardless of what they say about it, we are going to keep it."

It was a treacly, gag-inducing triumph that future generations of public figures would ape. The messages poured into Republican headquarters in Washington D.C., running some 350 to 1 in favor of Nixon. Ike kept him on the ticket, and never again gave serious thought to dumping him. Well, until 1956, at least.

THE NIX IS IN

Though he would live another eight years after leaving office, Dwight Eisenhower was not wholly in his prime during his Presidency, and the endless mornings and afternoons on the golf course did little to inspire confidence in his physical stature. With a heart attack in 1955 and surgery for ileitis in June of the next year, there was serious consideration that Richard Nixon could be a heartbeat or lower intestinal obstruction away from the Presidency. Eisenhower was also disappointed that Nixon's popularity hadn't improved during his first term in office, and that he was still regarded as little more than an attack dog. True to from, Ike kept his options open and remained coy

Fun Facts

Eisenhower wasn't a big help to Nixon's 1960 Presidential campaign. When asked about Nixon's contribution to the governance of the nation during his eight years as Ike's second-in-command, Ike said, "If you give me a week, I might think of one."

The infamous 1960 Presidential campaign wasn't the first time that Nixon and JFK met in a debate. The two had previously squared off in 1947, when both freshmen congressmen were selected to debate the Taft-Hartley Act at a public forum.

about keeping Nixon on the ticket for a second run, and even Nixon's old friend, Harold Stassen, stepped up with a "Dump Nixon" drive, citing polls that showed Ike would lose up to six points with Nixon on the ticket.

The Democrats seized the opportunity for some election-year fear mongering and cautioned that "the career and character of Richard Nixon pose a somber issue in the 1956 campaign." The again-nominee Adlai Stevenson all but started shoveling dirt on Ike's face by stating that "every piece of scientific evidence… indicates that a Republican victory would mean that Richard Nixon would probably be president of this country within the next four years."

In the end, Nixon toned down the scowl and the snarling, and Ike kept him onboard—though it was Nixon's self invitation to remain on the ticket that forced Ike's hand. The Vice President spent his second term carrying Administration water, arguing with Khrushchev in the fake kitchen, and preparing to be yet another in the long line of Vice Presidents since Martin Van Buren not to succeed his boss.

LIMA BEANED

In 1957, Dwight Eisenhower sent Vice President Nixon on a goodwill visit to Peru and several other South American countries. Their motorcade was assaulted in Caracas, Venezuela, to the point that the limo driver had to turn on the windshield wipers to clear away the spit that was coming from the crowd. Rocks broke the car's windows and cut Nixon and the Venezuelan foreign minister, and a Secret Service agent drew his revolver, resigning that if they were all going to die at the hands of this mob, then he was going to see how many he could take with them. Fortunately, the Vice President and his detail were able to escape the fracas before any serious bloodshed occurred.

Things were little better in Lima, Peru, where Nixon was greeted by a large crowd of young, enthusiastic Communists who pelted him with rocks. In an unorthodox effort to defuse the situation, Nixon called the crowd "the worst kind of cowards." The adulation from the locals continued outside Nixon's hotel, where the Vice President of the United States responded to a man who spat in his face by kicking him square in the shins.

 # LYNDON BAINES JOHNSON
DEMOCRAT, TEXAS
WITH JOHN F. KENNEDY, 1961–63

All things considered, 1960 was not a banner year for Lyndon Baines Johnson. He was entering his sixth very successful year as Senate Majority Leader, but he caught the bug and decided it was time for him to be President. Such was his faith in his power and the inevitability of his nomination that he remained on the job in D.C., leaving it to Hubert Humphrey and JFK to fight it out on the hustings while he would "stay here and mind the store." He planned on the nomination coming down to the convention where the delegates would select him overwhelmingly, and he could bring JFK onboard to balance the ticket and clean Richard Nixon's clock in November.

To the surprise of Johnson and everyone else, Kennedy pulled out a stunner in the West Virginia primary, and the delegates gave JFK the nomination on the first ballot. To the surprise of Kennedy and everyone else, Johnson accepted Kennedy's courtesy offer of the #2 spot on the ticket. "I didn't offer the Vice-Presidency to him," said JFK later. "I just held it out like this, and he grabbed at it."

Many said it made sense for Johnson, given the stresses of his job (he'd had a Texas-sized heart attack in 1955 that almost killed him, forcing him to reduce his workday from 18 to 14 hours) and that a growing number of liberal Democrats in the Senate threatened his reign as an effective Majority Leader. He could help deliver the South to the Democrats, and—elusive as it had been to past Vice Presidents—he was LBJ, and this could still be a step toward the White House. "Power is where power goes," he reasoned.

Still, by any measure, it was a step down. The party was less than united (the convention chairman tried to put LBJ's nomination through on a voice vote rather than a state-by-state vote, but it still didn't seem as if Johnson had enough "Ayes" in his favor, and the chair awkwardly gaveled for the nomination anyway). Many of LBJ's close friends and associates were incredulous. ("Who'd want to be Vice President for that man?" said one. Another friend, oilman and fellow Senator Robert S. Kerr, was slightly more exercised. "Get me my .38!" he yelled at LBJ, Lady Bird, and their friend Bobby Baker. "I'm gonna kill every damn one of you. I can't believe that my three best friends would betray me.")

*"I cannot stand Johnson's damn long face.
He comes in, sits at the cabinet meetings, with his face all
screwed up, never says anything. He looks so sad."*
—President Kennedy, complaining to George Smathers
about his clearly miserable Vice President.

On Election Night, Lyndon Baines Johnson appeared to hold little joy in seeing his new job become a reality. Had Joe Kennedy and Richard Daley not teamed up to bring home the great State of Cook County for JFK, Johnson could have kept his seat in Washington, thanks to the adoration of the Texas State legislature who allowed him to run simultaneously for the Vice Presidency and re-election to the Senate.

Instead, from a position where some historians have called him the best who ever held the post, Johnson took a job that most agreed was beneath him. In a note to Johnson, his friend, Senator Barry Goldwater, wrote simply, "I'm nauseated."

With JFK's assassination, LBJ did ascend to the Presidency, using Kennedy's post-mortem goodwill to pass much of his Great Society legislation, but the pull of Vietnam drew him closer and closer to—and finally down—the drain. He was reviled by much of the electorate, declined to run again for the Presidency, and left Washington for good in 1969. Returning to his Texas ranch with a renewed enthusiasm for alcohol and nicotine, he grew his hair long and lamented how the kids had been right before finally dying of a broken heart on January 22, 1973.

ASSAULT ON PRECINCT BOX 13

Johnson's victory in the 1948 U.S. Senate primary can most charitably be described as "curious." In a recount, Johnson emerged victorious by a margin of 87 votes. The election turned on 202 "found" votes from Precinct Box 13 in tiny Alice, Texas. A later examination of the votes—all but two cast for Johnson—would reveal that the names were added to the poll list in a handwriting and ink different from the originally counted votes, and all in alphabetical order. An election-night miracle!

Well, it wasn't quite so magical. Local election judge Luis Salas would tell many years later of a meeting in Alice with LBJ associate and local crony George Carr (known as "the Duke of Duval County" in Texas political circles). Carr said that LBJ was pleading for 200 more votes, so Carr ordered Salas to make it so. LBJ's supporters would deny this charge throughout and after his lifetime, but their defenses weren't always predicated on Johnson's inherent goodness. "He was much more devious than that," said one. Others were more shocked at the continued ballyhoo over this alleged "scandal." "Of course they stole that election," said a former LBJ aide. "That's the way they did it down there."

The *Texas Observer's* founding editor, Ronnie Dugger, interviewed LBJ in Texas near the end of his life. Dugger claimed that LBJ showed him a picture of five county officials posing with Precinct Box 13. When Dugger attempted further inquiries, LBJ only smiled. Years later, Dugger interviewed an aging Luis Salas, who produced the same photo.

AHMAD-IST PROPOSAL

Early in 1961, JFK sent his Vice President on a visit to Asia. Always the campaigner—and likely stuck with some leftover inventory from the previous election—Johnson popped into slums in India to hand out pencils reading, "Complements of your Senator, Lyndon Baines Johnson—the greatest good for the greatest number."

During a stop in Pakistan, Johnson heartily told a camel driver that if he were ever in the United States, "Y'all come and see us, ya heah?" Like the hundreds of other times he offered the throwaway courtesy, he likely forgot it immediately.

Bashir Ahmad, though, thought it was a splendid idea. He couldn't write or read, didn't speak a word of English, and arrived in New York City wearing shoes for the first time in his life. LBJ welcomed him warmly to the United States and took him for a stay on his ranch in Texas, with a brief stop in Kansas City to visit former President Truman. Johnson even made arrangements for Bashir to visit Mecca on his way back to Pakistan.

ORIFICE MEETING

Johnson distrusted, and in some cases despised, Kennedy's inner circle as much as they did him. After he assumed the Presidency, he delighted in dragging the occasional "delicate Kennedy-ite" into the bathroom with him to continue a meeting, even if he wasn't going in there to floss his teeth—or even empty his bladder. He had no qualms evacuating his bowels in front of anyone, but he took special pleasure in affronting the sensibilities of the Kennedy crowd who stayed on as aides and associates.

LAVATORY RAT

Not until Idaho Senator Larry Craig would a politician's identity be so intertwined with his bathroom behavior as Lyndon Baines Johnson's. Besides his aforementioned washroom summits, as a young Congressional aide in the 1930s Johnson rented a room at the Dodge Hotel in Washington D.C. There was one bathroom on his floor, and Johnson used the communal loo to do his first networking in this new and unfamiliar town, taking four showers and brushing his teeth five times in his first 24 hours to make as many Capitol connections as he possibly could.

Fun Facts

LBJ was very fond of his penis, naming it "Jumbo."

While probably no less fond of his dogs, he was less creatively inspired in choosing their names, "Him" and "Her."

LBJ died less than a month after Harry S Truman, leaving the United States with no living former Presidents until Richard Nixon reluctantly accepted the mantle on the afternoon of August 9, 1974.

Hubert Horatio Humphrey
Democrat, Minnesota
With Lyndon Baines Johnson, 1965–69

H ubert Humphrey had made a great splash with his firﬅ
dip in the public pool. As mayor of Minneapolis, he gave a
speech at the 1948 Democratic Convention railing againﬅ
the Democrats' safe, flaccid platform on civil rights, sending the
Southern delegates apopleﬅic when he declared, "My friends, to those
who say, that we are rushing this issue of civil rights, I say to them we
are 172 years too late!" Mississippi and half of the Alabama delegation
would walk out, and Senator Strom Thurmond would challenge
Truman as the firﬅ candidate of the Dixiecrat party. Of Humphrey,
one Southern Senator wondered aloud, "Can you imagine the people
of Minnesota sending that damn fool down here to represent them?"

Humphrey was eleﬅed to the Senate that year, and right out of
the gate he was uncompromising and made few friends. *Time* magazine said his critics thought him "Too cocky, too slick, too shallow, too
ambitious."

His fellow Class of '48 freshman, Lyndon Johnson, would slow
him down and teach him a little about Washington finesse. Humphrey
settled into a groove in D.C., and he and Johnson made a formidable
alliance through the 50s and beyond, as LBJ leaned heavily on the fiery
little man from Minnesota after JFK's assassination.

It was a foregone conclusion to moﬅ that LBJ would seleﬅ Hubert as his running mate in 1964. Johnson had made it clear, though,
that he wanted an ally and a facilitator for his agenda. As Humphrey
became confliﬅed about the Vietnam War, their relationship ﬅrained,
and Johnson's admiration for his close friend trended toward the ugly.
The President was none too happy when his VP equivocated about the
Johnson Agenda or wandered off the reservation entirely, and in ways
big and small, sublime and ridiculous, he made Humphrey pay.

Besides the occasional public humiliation, or pointedly ﬅaring at
his watch after ordering Humphrey to limit his Cabinet address to five
minutes and no more (and then pushing Humphrey out of the room
when his five minutes were up), Johnson never offered his endorsement of Humphrey's own Presidential bid in 1968, and the war protes-
tors crucified Humphrey for carrying Johnson's water on the war.

"If only I could breed him to Calvin Coolidge."
—LBJ, lamenting Humphrey's loquaciousness.

Humphrey lost a close race to a deeply unpopular Republican standard-bearer who would leave his own dubious mark on a Presidential tenure that should have been Humphrey's. Even though Hunter S. Thompson called Humphrey a "treacherous, gutless old ward-heeler" and said that "there is no way to grasp what a shallow, contemptible and hopelessly dishonest old hack Hubert Humphrey is until you've followed him around for a while," Hubert Humphrey was neither Richard Nixon (nor Spiro Agnew), and would likely have left the office in as good a position as when he assumed it, or at the very least sullied it less.

With the Presidency having handily eluded him lo these many years, Hubert Humphrey died in January 1978 with an extremely cancerous bladder. His body was only the 22nd to be displayed in the Capitol Rotunda.

PLEBE-ISCITE

Despite their history and their friendship—and that most of Washington assumed that LBJ was going to make Hubert Humphrey his running mate in 1964—Johnson wasn't about to just hand the prize to his friend and former colleague without a little executive-level hazing. LBJ led the press and Hubert along for an eternity, at one point during a State dinner loudly asking Humphrey what he thought of Senate President Mike Mansfield as a possible running mate. When Johnson finally invited Humphrey to Washington D.C. for what was surely his anointing as the Democratic Party's candidate for VP, he sent Humphrey's limo on an hour-long tour of D.C.'s most famous monuments and tourist attractions—never mind that Humphrey had been a creature of Washington since his election to the U.S. Senate in 1948.

Finally, Johnson allowed Humphrey's limousine onto the White House grounds—and proceeded to leave him waiting in the driveway for over an hour, where he eventually fell asleep, only to be shaken awake by Johnson, who would dismiss Humphrey's vexations at the belabored ritual by saying, "If you didn't know you were going to be Vice President a month ago, you're too damn dumb to have the office."

THE HUMPHREY BECOMES THE HUNTER

With a Y chromosome the size of his native Texas, Johnson never blanched at playing the macho card to shame a colleague or companion—either to get him to accede to his wishes, to size him up, or to clearly position himself as the alpha male. Despite his reputation as "the Happy Warrior" and for being an obstinate fighter when it came to civil rights, advocacy for the poor, and anti-Communism, Humphrey was the quintessential "doughy liberal" in many other regards.

Johnson once dragged Humphrey on a hunting trip with him. Approaching two deer, Johnson directed Humphrey to take the shot. Whereas later occupants of his office would have no problem using weapons against small animals and even their own hunting companions, Vice President Humphrey was clearly out of his element firing upon woodland creatures, and he balked at Johnson's directive. Having pulled the same tactic against Bobby Kennedy on an earlier hunting trip, Johnson used Kennedy's acquiescence to deride Humphrey to pull the trigger, lest anyone find out he wasn't as much of a man *as a Kennedy.*

Fun Facts

Musical humorist Tom Lehrer wrote a song about Vice President Humphrey entitled "Whatever Became of Hubert?"

At the 2004 Republican Convention, California Governor Arnold Schwarzenegger cited the 1968 Presidential debates between Richard Nixon and Vice President Humphrey as his moment of political awakening as a Republican. There were no debates between Nixon and Humphrey in 1968.

COWBERT

At his Texas ranch, Johnson on one occasion ordered the diminutive Minnesotan to dress in ill-fitting cowboy gear and a deliberately oversized ten-gallon hat, and then laughed with the assembled reporters as he marched the visibly awkward Humphrey in front of them. Johnson laughed even harder when his Vice President clumsily tried to climb onto an overanxious horse, which soon gave Humphrey perhaps the most terrifying ride of his life.

Spiro T. Agnew
Republican, Maryland
With Richard M. Nixon, 1969–73

While the Las Vegas line on Richard Nixon's probable Vice Presidential nominee leading up to the 1968 GOP Convention in Miami has likely been lost to history, you could guess that the smart money was going toward either Governor Ronald Reagan, New York Governor Nelson Rockefeller, or maybe New York City Mayor John Lindsay. Strong horses picking up the rear included Massachusetts Governor John Volpe, Maryland Congressman Rogers Morton, and Tennessee Senator Howard Baker. Then, further down the list (much, much further down the list— probably amidst the likes of Tiny Tim, Tommy Smothers, and Señor Wences), one would have found the name of Maryland's Governor, Spiro T. Agnew.

For a man who had reached the apex of a long climb back from political oblivion, Richard Nixon's first proclamation from atop the mountain was a vexing one. Of all the heavyweights in the Republican party who could have brought different strengths to the ticket, Nixon chose a first-term Governor not even two years removed from that much coveted seat of power, the Baltimore County Board of Appeals. For most of that Thursday, August 8, the mantra "Spiro who?" reverberated through the Miami Beach Convention Center.

Nixon had his reasons, not the least of which was that he wanted a "political eunuch" and not a party superstar who might outshine him. And since his election two years earlier, Agnew had remade himself from a moderate/liberal into a snarling scold who could draw hard-line votes away from George Wallace and Curtis LeMay. On the campaign trail he didn't disappoint, showing his cultural diversity with such Big Tent declarations as "If you've seen one city slum, you've seen them all" and "Very frankly, when I'm moving in a crowd, I don't look and say, 'Well, there's a Negro, there's an Italian, and there's a Greek and there's a Polack.'"

But perhaps Nixon's strongest reason for his choice of running mate was revealed when he commented variously that Agnew was his insurance against being assassinated or impeached, as no one wanted to see Spiro Agnew in the White House.

"He is not fit to stand one step away from the Presidency."
—*New York Times* editorial

They won the election in a squeaker over Hubert Humphrey and Edmund Muskie, but the Nixon-Agnew Presidency would come to an unseemly, ignominious end on August 8th six years later, when the disgraced President announced he would be following his disgraced Vice President out the door. Camelot, this wasn't.

ALL THOSE OPPOSED SAY "NEIGH"

The *Washington Post* opined in a Summer 1968 editorial that Nixon's selection of Agnew was "perhaps the most eccentric political appointment since Caligula named his horse a consul."

TEE THE PEOPLE

An avid golfer, Agnew participated in the 1970 Bob Hope Chrysler Classic in Southern California. Bruce Devlin won the tournament that year, hitting a 339—21 strokes under par. Elsewhere on the leader board, Vice President Agnew hit three spectators in the gallery and bounced a drive off his partner's skull.

WELL-PLAYED, GOV'NOR!

A onetime friend of Agnew, Oregon's outspoken Governor Tom McCall quickly bristled at many of the newly elevated Vice President's comments. One month after the 1968 election, Agnew was invited to a Republican governors' convention in Sun Valley, Idaho. Leading up to the meeting, McCall denounced Agnew in the press as the President's "hatchet man... a triggerman... like a man with a knife in his shawl." At the conference, Agnew delivered a biting, partisan speech, leading McCall to walk out of the meeting room in the middle of Agnew's address, soon after telling reporters, "There was the most unbelievable, incredible misunderstanding of the mood of America in that rotten, bigoted little speech." Later, an incensed Agnew met face-to-face with McCall to dress him down for his comments. "Tom, I can't believe you said this!" Agnew bellowed, waving a copy of the morning paper in McCall's face.

"What does it say?" McCall asked, feigning innocence.

Agnew pointed at the paper, reminding McCall that he described the Vice President's address as a "rotten, bigoted little speech."

McCall nodded, but, defending himself against Agnew's accusation, corrected, "I don't think I said 'little.'"

HE WASN'T *THAT* FAT

On his campaign plane after an event in Las Vegas, Governor Agnew noticed *Baltimore Sun* reporter Gene Oishi sleeping off a night at the casino, and asked the other assembled reporters, "What's wrong with the fat Jap?" To Agnew's great offense, the remark was reported. Agnew claimed that he was cordial with Oishi and had been kidding, and just to drive the point home, continued on the campaign trail to greet Oishi with a jovial, "How's the fat Jap today?"

SUPPLEMENTAL INCOME

All its surface glamour notwithstanding, it's not easy to make ends meet as a government worker. This was the predicament Spiro Agnew found himself facing as Baltimore County Executive, Governor of Maryland, and even when he moved into the West Wing.

It was lucky for Spiro that he had friends like Lester Matz willing to help him pay the bills and keep him in walking-around money. Or at least it was until a federal grand jury subpoenaed his engineering firm's records to determine if he was sending kickbacks to county officials on some public works projects. Matz was willing to confess to this unsavory arrangement, but it was a little more complicated than that: He was also giving kickbacks to the Vice President of the United States. Wait. What?

From the time that Agnew was Baltimore County Executive, Agnew helped send government contracts Matz's way in exchange for a modest 5% of the value of each contract. It was apparently a fruitful arrangement for both, as it continued after Agnew was elected governor. On one occasion, in fact, Matz delivered an envelope filled with $20,000 in cash to Agnew at his statehouse office in Annapolis. Such is the nature of these contracts, it's often years before all of the terms are fulfilled, the projects completed, and the stipulated monies paid. It was for this reason that at one point in Agnew's first term as Vice President, Matz visited Agnew in his basement office at the White House, where he presented the Vice President of the United States with an envelope containing $10,000 in cash, which Matz says Agnew slipped into his desk drawer. Matz said that the dubious tree they had grown together might yet bear more fruit. Agnew was happy to oblige him. If Matz desired another meeting, he merely had to call Agnew's secretary and state that he had more "information" to share with the VP.

As "Get Out Of Jail Free" cards go, they don't get much bigger than the one Matz and his attorney were holding. They contacted the U.S. Attorney in Baltimore, who would subsequently contact new

United States Attorney General Elliott Richardson to negotiate an immunity deal for Matz in exchange for full disclosure of his arrangement with Vice President Agnew. For 35-year-old U.S. Attorney George Beall, who was already investigating kickbacks to Agnew's successor in the Maryland statehouse, this was a very good day for his career, as he had the honor of informing Richardson that there might be something of a succession crisis brewing.

As summer turned to fall, there was a proliferation of witnesses and box upon box upon box of evidence, and still more witnesses who reported that Agnew had received money as governor and after he was elected Vice President, often taking delivery in his office in the Old Senate Office Building. It was obvious that the case against the Vice President was simply too strong, and Agnew was well beyond the point of righteous indignation or demanding that his name be cleared. The only option that remained for him was his endgame, and—if at all possible—keeping himself out of prison.

Finally, after much back and forth, on the evening of October 8, 1973, Spiro Agnew met Richard Nixon at the White House and announced his intention to be the second Vice President in the history of the United States to tender his resignation. With the same resourcefulness he showed in supplementing his government salary with what one could charitably describe as the "finder's fees" he received

Fun Facts

Showing his intimate knowledge of America, Agnew made a trip to Chicago in the great state he referred to as *"Illi-noise."*

In his memoir *"Go Quietly…Or Else,"* Agnew implies that Nixon and Alexander Haig were plotting to have him assassinated if he didn't voluntarily resign from the Vice Presidency.

Haig didn't trust Agnew either, telling his wife that if he disappeared, she "might want to look inside any recently poured concrete bridge pilings in Maryland."

from Lester Matz and others, Agnew made one last request of his
President before he resigned: Was there a foreign assignment that
might be suitable, or did the President know of a corporation who was
looking for a loyal, industrious individual with executive branch experience who would be invaluable as a consultant? It was certainly worth
a try, but the President apparently demurred, as Agnew the next day
had his lawyers deliver his resignation to the Secretary of State's office.

Agnew ultimately plead no contest to one count of tax evasion
and money laundering, and he was placed on three years probation
and ordered to pay a $10,000 fine. He was disbarred by the State of
Maryland and played out his last years as a well-paid consultant, even
dabbling in bad fiction (check out his 1980 potboiler, *The Canfield
Decision*, about a Vice President "destroyed by his own ambition"). On
September 17, 1996, Agnew visited the hospital, and it was discovered
that he had leukemia. He was dead within a few hours.

GERALD R. FORD
REPUBLICAN, MICHIGAN
WITH RICHARD M. NIXON, 1973–74

After winning election to his 13th term in the House of Representatives and his fifth as House Minority Leader, Gerald Ford planned to run for one more term before hanging it up in January 1977. He would indeed retire in January 1977, but it would be as President of the United States, his second job in the Executive Branch, having served ten months as Vice President before that, appointed by Nixon and approved by Congress after Spiro Agnew resigned in disgrace.

Unexpected, but it all worked out for the best. He was a member of not one, but two very exclusive clubs: one of only 15 men in American history to serve as Vice President and President, and the first non-elected member of both. He was immortalized on one of the most popular shows on television and made headlines when two lunatic women in seventeen days tried to kill him. When he retired from government, he had Secret Service protection for life and got his own library. When he died, remembrances filled the television, magazines, and newspapers for a week. That's a whole lot of hoopla for a friendly, uncontroversial, porridge-bland Congressman from Grand Rapids, who made it nearly 25 years in the House without writing a single piece of legislation.

"I am a Ford, not a Lincoln."
—Newly sworn Vice President
Gerald Ford's inaugural address.

He may well have earned his own term had he not decided one month into his Presidency to squander all of his post-Watergate goodwill on one lazy Sunday morning by pardoning Richard Nixon, who was still facing lengthy investigations, a trial, and possible jail time. Cries of "quid pro quo" went up across the country, and Ford's approval ratings sank almost as precipitously as Nixon's had.

OH, *"DOMI*NATION." SORRY

Whatever damage that Ford's colleagues' anecdotal descriptions did to his intellectual reputation was a shaving nick compared to the evisceration Ford inflicted upon himself in his biggest gaffe ever. In the 1976 Presidential debate with Georgia governor Jimmy Carter, Ford offered—despite the looming presence of the Cold War and the Warsaw Pact on American and world politics and life—"There is no Soviet domination of Eastern Europe, nor will there be during a Ford administration." Residents of Poland, Romania, and Bulgaria would not have been wrong to wonder if they'd missed a memo had they heard Ford continue to defend his assertion in post-debate interviews. Many claim that this was a fatal blow to the Ford campaign in what was a very close race.

"FORRRRRRRRRD!"

Serving in the White House under Richard Nixon wasn't the only thing Gerald Ford and Spiro Agnew had in common. Ford was such an errant golfer that he found his way into Bob Hope's material. (Gerald Ford…"the man who made golf a contact sport." "You all know Jerry Ford—the most dangerous driver since *Ben Hur*"… "Ford is easy to spot on the course. He drives the cart with the red cross painted on top." etc.) He sliced into the spectators' gallery several times and once hit a woman in the head. Ford himself would later quip, "I know I'm getting better at golf because I'm hitting fewer spectators." In *First Off The Tee*, writer Don Van Natta, Jr. says of Ford, "He hit many, many people with golf balls." Van Natta blames this on Ford's tendency to play events where there were spectator galleries on both sides of the fairway.

READY FOR HIS CLOSEUP

Ford dated a model in the 1940s before he met his current wife, Betty. Through this liaison, he secured enough modeling contacts that he was able to find gainful employment in the field for a time. Somewhere among the musty magazine stacks across America, you can still find the man we've come to know as a bald, bumbling, lovable oaf striking a steamy pose on the April 1942 cover of *Cosmopolitan*.

PRESIDUNCE IN WAITING

Though he died some months before Ford would make the last remarkable ascents of his political career, the man who preceded him in both offices would have been unlikely to offer his endorsement. LBJ once famously commented that Ford "played too much football without a helmet" and "can't fart and chew gum at the same time." When Ford was House Minority Leader in 1965, LBJ was hoping for his help in passing a bill that was coming before Congress. LBJ directed one of his aides, who had a young son, to visit the Capitol with some of the child's toy blocks and "explain to Jerry Ford what we're trying to do."

Fun Facts

Quite the football player in his youth, Ford received offers to play for both the Detroit Lions and Green Bay Packers. He turned down both to coach the football team at Yale.

Ford served on the Warren Commission on John F. Kennedy's assassination and altered the first draft of the report, so that the path of the bullet into Kennedy supported the Single Bullet Theory.

 # NELSON ALDRICH ROCKEFELLER
REPUBLICAN, NEW YORK
WITH GERALD FORD, 1974–77

T hough many men of substantial means have entered politics for reasons of posterity or supplemental financial enrichment, anyone at all familiar with the Rockefeller lineage knows that Nelson Aldrich Rockefeller had no reason to heed the call of public service. Yet he served many years in the arena, first as an unlikely and sometimes unconvincing populist, and later as a sop to the right wing of his party, an unlikely and scarily convincing hardliner (including the nasty "Rockefeller Drug Laws"—which equated possession of four ounces or more of certain narcotics with second-degree murder—and his response to the Attica Prison, riots which resulted in the deaths of 39 inmates and hostages after a breakdown in negotiations between authorities and the inmates holding the prison).

After a successful turn running the family business, Rockefeller served a number of appointments for FDR (who'd appointed Rockefeller to blunt his support for opponent Wendell Willkie), Truman (who fired him), and Eisenhower, before catching the eye of his party by winning the New York Statehouse in a very un-Republican year. From that point forward he was always considered presidential timber. He was courted as the anti-Nixon in '60, sullied his chances in '64 because of an untimely marital trade-in for a younger model (followed by the birth of their child), and was even courted by LBJ as the anti-Nixon and the anti-Humphrey in '68. Most of his energies, though, went into a long, busy, and mostly successful 14 years running New York State, where he presided over a building, education, and public works boom (helped in part by legislature and bureaucracy whose loyalty was encouraged by considerable "donations" from the deep pockets of the Governor). Eventually stepping aside to let his lieutenant governor serve two years so that he could run as an incumbent, Rockefeller began planning his 1976 Presidential bid.

Rockefeller had twice refused a chance at the Vice Presidency, but with the Nixon Administration imploding and Spiro Agnew implicated in accepting bags of money in shady deliveries in the White House basement, Rockefeller was suddenly interested again. After all, there was no telling how long Nixon would be around, and this might be a convenient shot at the brass ring without the messy and expensive

*"Copious in all things, Nelson in the end
produced a sixty-minute gap, where Nixon
couldonly manage eighteen and a half."*
—*The Washington Post*, comparing the suspicious
circumstances of Rockefeller's death to the demise of
Richard Nixon's Presidency.

chore of campaigning. But as it turned out, Nixon wanted Treasury Secretary John Connally, and the Congress gave him Gerald Ford.

When it was Ford's turn, however, after an exhaustive survey process involving every government official except the city council of Muncie, Indiana, Ford ordered background checks run on three candidates: RNC Chairman George H.W. Bush, Ford transition chairman Donald Rumsfeld, and Nelson Rockefeller.

It wasn't the pinnacle of Rockefeller's career that he'd imagined. He was just as marginalized as most of his predecessors (thanks in part to now Chief of Staff Donald Rumsfeld, who disagreed with his President letting the VP field the majority of domestic issues). "I go to funerals, I go to earthquakes," Rockefeller said. He went through the motions and tried to do what he could, even spending his own money for a redesign of the Vice Presidential seal. He vented to an aide one day, "See that goddamn seal? That's the most important thing I've done all year."

Ford dumped Rockefeller from the ticket in 1976 in favor of Kansas Senator Robert Dole. It was not Ford's proudest hour, as he would later confess. "It was the biggest political mistake of my life. And it was one of the few cowardly things I did in my life."

FAUX POPULI

It's always a dicey proposition when insulated millionaires have to pretend they comprehend the everyday lives of the Great Unwashed. When he rolled up his sleeves and jumped into elective politics, Rockefeller had no shortage of his own disconnected moments. During one speech, he attempted to make a point about the plight of the working class by saying, "Now you take an average family with an income of $100,000..." On another occasion, while serving as Governor, his aides discussed with him a plan for the state to cover Social Security contributions for state workers, so that they would have more take-home pay. "What is take-home pay?" he asked.

CHICK CHICK BOOM!

Nelson Rockefeller almost became President twice in the span of 17 days. On September 5, 1975, Ford was in Sacramento when a woman pointed a Colt-45 at him. She was thwarted by a Secret Service agent, who grabbed the gun and managed to jam the hammer with his hand. The woman was Charles Manson acolyte Lynnette "Squeaky" Fromme. ("Who is Manson?" asked the always ear-to-the-ground Vice President, when informed of the incident.)

On September 22, in San Francisco, another woman named Sara Jane Moore actually got off a shot, which was deflected by a former marine who happened to be standing near her. Moore had drawn the attention of the Secret Service earlier in the year, but in one of those unfortunate decisions that usually ends someone's career, it was determined that she posed no danger to the President.

"I DON'T KNOW... SOMETHING ABOUT A SLED"

Always besieged by money for this project or that cause, Nelson told an aide that once he had funded a movie simply because he'd tired of the director's pleading and wanted him out of his office. The nuisance director was Orson Welles, who was seeking financing for *Citizen Kane*. Rockefeller never saw the movie.

CORPUS ERECTI

Nelson Rockefeller's second wife, Happy, probably wasn't so at the circumstances surrounding his death. On January 26, 1979, Nelson Aldrich Rockefeller suffered a heart attack while reportedly having sexual intercourse with one Meagan Marshak, with whom he was supposedly having a business meeting (though the office was suspiciously bereft of papers and other business-like things). The heart attack allegedly occurred somewhere between 9:15 and 10:15 PM, but an ambulance wasn't called until 11:15 PM. Reports vary, but it was apparently a very busy hour or two at the Rockefeller suite, as aides scurried to "tidy up" the scene before police photographers arrived. According to Presidential historian Doris Kearns Goodwin, the aides dressed the en flagrante Rockefeller and sat him up in his chair, slumped over with a newspaper in his hands. They were apparently in a bit of a rush, however, as they left him for the police and paramedics with the newspaper upside down and his shoes on the wrong feet.

Much was made of the delay in calling for medical help for the stricken former Vice President. The family and estate eventually acknowledged the affair, and the cause of Rockefeller's death was officially classified as a heart attack suffered during sexual intercourse. When Rockefeller's will was read, it was revealed that he deeded Megan Marshak a New York town house and $50,000.

Fun Facts

Rockefeller was sworn in before the same cameras in the Senate chamber that had been installed to film Richard Nixon's impeachment hearings. After filming Rockefeller's inauguration in December 1974, there were no cameras in the Senate chamber until 1985.

Happier in his own expansive and expensive digs, Rockefeller spent only one night in the brand new Vice Presidential mansion commissioned by Congress.

WALTER F. MONDALE
DEMOCRAT, MINNESOTA
WITH JIMMY CARTER, 1977-81

W hile opinions may vary, by any objective measure of Jimmy Carter's Presidency, it's safe to say that he'll never be a candidate for the fifth face on Mount Rushmore. Hostages, gas lines, double-digit inflation, rampant unemployment, the energy crisis, Three Mile Island, malaise—that's not an America over which any President would have been proud to preside. In one act, though, he outshone nearly all his predecessors: He picked a competent Vice President and actually put him to good, constructive use.

For all of Carter's faults, he was neither insecure nor a megalomaniac. He had the novel idea that since the Vice President was a paid government employee and the holder of the second-highest elective office in the country, he should be capable and have a meaningful job description.

Unlike most of the men who preceded him in office, Walter Mondale was smart, competent, deliberate, honest, candid, and loyal, but not to a fault. He never had embarrassments that showed up on the nightly news or in the weekly newsmagazines. Shadowy men never brought him envelopes of cash in the White House basement. He was allowed extensive counsel with the President, and he was never sent off to the four corners of the world just because the U.S. needed a photo op and the President didn't want to risk contracting malaria or having rocks thrown at his motorcade. While the question was never posed as such in any mid-term poll, it's likely that more Americans feared

Fun Facts

Mondale is mentioned in three episodes of *The Simpsons*, most memorably as the namesake of the U.S. Navy's "laundry ship," the USS *Mondale*.

With a nod to a famous American automaker's slogan, Twin Cities Public Television produced a 1979 documentary on Vice President Mondale's visit to his ancestral Norway entitled *Walter Mondale: There's a Fjord in Your Past*.

"I'd have to set my hair on fire to get on the news."
—Vice President Mondale, on the campaign trail, 1980.

Jimmy Carter being a heartbeat away from the Presidency than Walter Mondale.

Perhaps this was his misfortune, because history will also remember Walter Mondale as one of the most benign, boring, unglamorous men ever to hold public office. Put another way, when people think of Minnesota's political legends, Hubert Humphrey is the dashing, sexy one.

BLAND SABBATH

During a college speaking tour in 1988, and on his spoken-word album *No More Cocoons*, Dead Kennedys lead singer Jello Biafra read a list of amusing potential band names that were begging to be put to use. One of the crowd favorites on the list was "Mondale!" Indeed, how better to communicate the angry disenfranchisement and devil-may-care hedonism of a lost generation than invoking the name of that mildest of Minnesotans, the 42nd Vice President of the United States.

ELECTORAL DYSFUNCTION

Running on his own as the Democratic nominee for President in 1984, Mondale was no match charismatically for Ronald Reagan, who brilliantly answered 56-year-old Mondale's insinuations that 73-year-old Reagan was too old to be President by saying, "I will not make age an issue of this campaign. I am not going to exploit, for political purposes, my opponent's youth and inexperience." Mondale won only his home state (by a scant 3,761 votes) and the District of Columbia, garnering 13 electoral votes and suffering the worst defeat for a Democratic Presidential candidate in the 20th century.

George H.W. Bush
Republican, Texas
With Ronald Reagan, 1981–89

or a man who flew 58 combat missions in World War II and was shot down twice before finally being ordered home, it's somewhat surprising that George Herbert Walker Bush's skeletal fortitude would be so challenged in his Vice Presidential years. This was, after all, the same George Bush who, as head of the Republican National Committee, stood up in the middle of a cabinet meeting and told Richard Nixon he should resign for the good of the country. After a spirited battle with Ronald Reagan for the 1980 GOP Presidential nomination in which he beat the former California Governor in the Iowa caucuses and assailed Reagan's "voodoo economics," George Bush folded his cards and surrendered his independence, his backbone, and his dignity to the Gipper for the next eight years. In 1984, *Doonesbury* cartoonist Garry Trudeau began portraying Bush as a disembodied voice and suggested in a Roland Hedley report that "to shelter what remains of his convictions, Bush is about to formally place his political manhood in a blind trust."

He took a slightly different, but no less unflattering strategy in 1987 when he denied involvement in—or knowledge of—the Iran-Contra Scandal by insisting, "I was out of the loop." Former Reagan Secretary of State Alexander Haig made hay of Bush's absence during the 1988 campaign, asking, "Where was George Bush during the story? Was he the copilot in the cockpit, or was he back in economy class?"

It was a very different George Bush who'd come into New Hampshire in 1980 with "the Big Mo" (which would be "momentum" to those not versed in Bushspeak), only to be shellacked in a public-ity coup by a much more media-savvy Ronald Reagan. With a debate sponsored by the *Nashua Telegraph* to which only Bush and Reagan were invited, the other candidates raised a stink and demanded they be allowed to participate, claiming that the forum in essence gave unfair advantage to Bush and Reagan. After Bush reluctantly agreed to Reagan's suggestion that the campaigns split the cost of the debate— and believing that he was still going mano a mano with the former Governor—Reagan blindsided Bush by magnanimously inviting the other candidates to participate. Bush was furious and dumbstruck, but

"I have strong reservations about George Bush.
I'm concerned about turning over the country to him."
—Ronald Reagan, on his eventual Vice President, 1980.

it was high theater from the actor-candidate as Reagan led the also-rans up to the stage and began to make the case for their participation. The moderator, Jon Breen, ordered Reagan's microphone shut off when Reagan thundered defiantly, "Mr. Green (sic)… I'm paying for this microphone." (Creature of Hollywood that he was, Reagan had lifted the line almost verbatim from Spencer Tracy's 1948 film, *State Of The Union*.)

Reagan looked a bold champion of American Democracy and The Everyman. Bush, steam coming off his ears, looked petulant and foolish. Except for a Bush victory in Michigan, Reagan sailed to the nomination. From that moment forward, George Bush began to realize that the road to his own White House would require time served in the Vice Presidency. It was transparent to his friends. "He's submerged his own views," said former Maryland Senator Charles Mathias. "The question is whether they have survived and will they surface?"

To bona fide conservatives who were already skeptical of him, it reeked of something worse. Wrote columnist George Will, "The unpleasant sound Bush is emitting as he traipses from one conservative gathering to another is a thin, tiny 'arf'—the sound of a lapdog." Indeed, it was all a rather unvarnished and unseemly display of ambition. He denied having used the "voodoo economics" line until he was confronted with a tape recording of it. The erstwhile moderate and abortion-rights supporter shamelessly praised Jerry Falwell, saying, "America is in crying need of the moral vision you have brought to our political life." Shortly before the 1984 election, he announced with pride, "I'm for Mr. Reagan, blindly."

Naked ambition is never a particularly attractive quality, even in a politician from whom one would expect nothing less. Bush sublimated a lifetime of conviction and a hard-earned reputation of being his own man to make his way to the top, and became the most compliant and seemingly unnecessary Vice President of the last half-century.

"But it all worked, didn't it?" said a veteran Bush aide who worked for Bush's campaign in 1988.

"PLEASE HELP ME SURVIVE THIS ORDEAL, LORD. I NEED FOOD AND WATER, A RESCUE BOAT, AND AN ORIGINAL COPY OF THE TREATY OF GREENVILLE..."

George Bush put off college to fight in World War II. Enlisting in the Navy at age 18, Bush became an ace carrier pilot—the youngest flight trainee in the American armed services. He lost four planes in the process, each named "Barbie" after the future First Lady. On one occasion, he was shot down over the Pacific near a Japanese-held island. He successfully ejected from the plane, but hit his head on the plane's tail. He managed to iwnflate a small life raft and stay afloat while avoiding capture. Having much time for reflection, he would later say in a speech at the Old Creamery Theater in Garrison, Ohio, "I thought of my family, my mom and dad, and the strength I got from them." Maybe the sun and the salt water also got to him—or maybe he just ran out of things to think about—because he added that he also pondered "the separation of church and state."

Fun Facts

On a trip to Dallas in 1981, Bush dedicated a memorial at the hotel where JFK had stayed before he had been murdered. While there, he learned of Reagan's attempted assassination in Washington D.C. by John Hinckley.

Despite an ugly, bruising, and very personal 1992 Presidential campaign, George Bush and Bill Clinton in the early 21st century would form one of the most unexpected friendships/father-son relationships in modern memory. (Barbara Bush has even referred to Clinton by saying *"I have another son who was President."*)

DEBUTIZED

Despite all of the anointing and the formidable campaign fund he'd amassed, Bush ſtumbled in his firſt teſt in the 1988 campaign, limping to a feeble third-place finish in the Iowa caucuses, behind snarling Kansas Senator Bob Dole and acclaimed lunatic Reverend Pat Robertson. Bush flew his Connecticut/Maine colors when he wrote it off to the unfortunate timing. "A lot of people…were at their daughters' coming-out parties." Because, of course, it's well known that Saturdays in January are the height of the Iowa debutante season.

HOT FOR GIPPER

During the campaign of 1988, Bush ſtarted to take ſteps to diſtance himself from Ronald Reagan—not to disparage his benefactor and mentor, but to appear as his "own man." Speaking to a group of reporters, Bush responded to a queſtion about his relationship with President Reagan: "For seven and a half years I've worked alongside President Reagan. We've had triumphs. Made some miſtakes. We've had some sex… setbacks."

"KEEP WALKING, AND DON'T MAKE EYE CONTACT—YOU'LL ONLY ENCOURAGE HIM"

A group of international touriſts was walking through Washington D.C.'s Lafayette Park when they were suddenly confronted with the bizarre spectacle of a man shouting at them, "Hey, hey, nihaoma. Hey, yeah, yeah. Heil, heil—a kind of Hitler salute." It's hard to imagine who appeared more unsettled that Sunday morning—the touriſts being confronted with this odd salutation, or the well-meaning, Labrador-like leader of the United States, George Bush, who was delivering it. "Nihaoma," incidentally, is Mandarin for "how are you?"

J. Danforth Quayle
Republican, Indiana
With George H.W. Bush, 1989–93

F or what was supposed to be the year of his political apogee, 1988 was not starting well for George Herbert Walker Bush. With no less than 14 other competitors vying to succeed Ronald Reagan—and five of those from his own party—the crosshairs were already trained on the would-be heir apparent, Vice President Bush. History served as a 15ᵗʰ competitor, in that no sitting Vice President since Martin Van Buren had won election to the Presidency.

Bush thought he'd paid his dues, but imagine his surprise when he was trounced in Iowa by his nemesis, Senator Robert Dole of Kansas, and by firebrand *700 Club* televangelist Reverend Pat Robertson as well.

If it hadn't been for a comeback in New Hampshire—thanks to Bush's friend, Governor John Sununu, and a last-minute ad blitz savaging Dole, that February night in Manchester could have spelled the end of the Bush Dynasty.

With his high-profile vanquishing of Bob Dole, his new cutthroat political team, and the apparent shedding of the dreaded "wimp factor," Bush seemed ready to reclaim the backbone he'd surrendered when he became Ronald Reagan's running mate eight years earlier. For that reason more than any other, all eyes were on New Orleans in August 1988 for Bush to cap the GOP convention with his first Presidential decision—his choice of a running mate.

Bush's image, both in the popular press and by his own neverending stream of verbal gaffes, beset the Vice President and his aides with a significant quandary—how to hit a homerun with his first executive decision by choosing a bright star from the firmament, but not someone so bright that they would outshine Bush himself. There was no shortage of bona fide heavyweights—Congressman Jack Kemp, Senator Alan Simpson of Wyoming, his bitter rival Bob Dole, Elizabeth Dole, Tennessee Governor Lamar Alexander, etc., were all powerhouses within their party who stood large on their own two feet. But there was one fellow—a young Senator from Indiana…

In the days leading up to Bush's announcement, politicos were incredulous at the rumors that J. Danforth Quayle was actually on Bush's short list. He'd shown up on a long list of possible choices,

"I stand by all the misstatements that I've made."
—Quayle in an interview with ABC's Sam Donaldson,
August 17, 1989.

but the prevailing belief among the pundits and politicians in New Orleans for the 1988 Republican Convention was that the 41-year-old, second-term junior Senator from Indiana was included as a "decoy" to muddy the waters and draw attention away from the heavyweight candidates that Bush was considering.

A reasonable enough assumption. This was a big decision, and Bush was going to do it right. After all he'd endured, after all the obstacles he'd overcome, after all those years when his manhood and judgment and intelligence were questioned, now that he'd claimed the mantle of leadership in the Republican Party, there was no way he'd possibly shoot himself in the foot and choose for his running mate this doughy, serially golfing publishing heir who was nicknamed "Wet Head" during his first years in Congress because on the occasions when he did manage to make it to the Senate, he always appeared to be coming from the gym. Would he?

Well…his chief political consultant, Roger Ailes, had advised the Vice President to "throw a few long balls" leading up to the convention. With Dan Quayle (also, coincidentally, an Ailes client; in fact, Ailes was the only adviser in Bush's circle to have Quayle anywhere near the top of his short list), Bush lofted one over the end zone and up into the nosebleeds. Making their way to join Bush on the paddle boat *Natchez* for the announcement, Dan and Marilyn Quayle looked like just another anonymous, anodyne young Republican couple there to join in the festivities, barely making it through the crowd to join the Candidate.

Quayle was indeed the choice, stunning much of the world, to whom a giddy, buoyant Danny Quayle excitedly introduced himself by grabbing Bush in a clumsy, jarring embrace and announcing, "Let's go get 'em! All right? You got it?" prompting Quayle's new handler, Stuart Spencer, to note, "Well, we gotta correct that."

NO WAY TO HUNT QUAYLE

1984 Reagan-Bush campaign manager, Ed Rollins, complained that the Bush running mate selection process was flawed from the beginning. Bush sent one of his closest confidants, onetime appointed U.S. Senator from New Jersey, Nick Brady, to visit his former colleagues in the Senate and ask them how they felt about Dan Quayle being Bush's running mate. Bush was not only the sitting Vice President at the time, but likely the future President. As Rollins rightly pointed out, since their opinion was being solicited by a staunch Bush ally, they couldn't be counted on for their candor and objectivity. "You could take any group of political people in this town… and say, 'Hey, what do you think of Dan Quayle? I'm really serious about putting him on the ticket.' There wouldn't be a person in the room stand up (for Quayle)."

During the campaign, future George H.W. Bush press secretary Torie Clarke took Senator John McCain to task for a comment he'd made that Dan Quayle would help with women voters. McCain told Clarke, "Torie, I know three things about Dan Quayle: He's dumber than shit, he's a scratch golfer, and he's good-looking. I went with his strengths."

"POGO POGO"

Shortly after Bush and Quayle were inaugurated, Bush sent his new Vice President on a 12-day tour of the Far East, starting in the Pacific. It seemed a low-risk opportunity to test-drive Quayle's diplomacy skills—a harmless round of photo opportunities and "meet-n-greets" with America's most non-controversial allies, and then they'd give him remedial training afterwards as needed. Quayle's first stop was in Hawaii, where Air Force II was to be refueled. His initial informal address fell somewhat short of the dignity one would expect from a representative of America's Executive Branch of government, but did offer penetrating insights into Hawaii's place in the world: "Hawaii has always been a very pivotal role in the Pacific. It is in the Pacific. It is a part of the United States that is an island that is right here." Frank and guileless, well-intentioned, but definitely not controversial.

If only that could be said about his next stop in American Samoa. In Pago Pago, which is pronounced "Pango Pango," Quayle made his first misstep, pronouncing the capital, "Pogo Pogo." Awkward, but not fatal. Unfortunately, he would continue speaking during his visit, addressing the locals: "Keep that commitment to just being happy people… But you all look like happy campers to me. Happy campers

you are. Happy campers you have been. And, as far as I am concerned, happy campers you will always be."

After Quayle's visit, the territory's Congressional delegate, Eni F.H. Faleomavaega, issued a letter of protest at Quayle's remarks, saying, "It appears that some individuals have even drawn the conclusion that the people of Samoa are simple, illiterate natives happily camped out in the jungle."

I PUT A SPELL ON YOU

Dan Quayle's problems with the English language did not just manifest themselves verbally. Several embarrassing artifacts and incidents from his time on the public stage helped cement his reputation as one of our least literate Vice Presidents, from the Christmas card he and Marilyn sent out in 1989 ("May our nation continue to be the beakon of hope to the world") to the stationery found in 1993 by incoming Clinton staffers, with the letterhead, "Office of the Vice President... The Council on Competativeness." There was also his note to golfing legend Sam Snead after the two shared a round of golf in 1991: "Sam, had a great time this weekend but the golf was lousey."

But none of these revelations were as damaging and widely reported as Quayle's June 15, 1992 visit to Munoz Rivera School in Trenton, New Jersey. After a day of education-related speeches and appearances, Quayle arrived at the school and was eventually escorted into a classroom for a planned spelling bee. Quayle was to read words off flash cards and direct students to attempt to spell them correctly on the chalkboard. An aide asked if anyone "checked the cards."

"Oh, yeah," said advance man Keith Nahigian. "We looked at them and they're just very simple words. No big deal." And so the stage was set. With cameras poised to capture the photo opportunity, Vice President Quayle stood by with the instructor as 12-year-old William Figueroa stepped to the front of the class to receive his word. Quayle read the word, and William spelled out on the chalkboard: "P-O-T-A-T-O."

Quayle politely corrected the boy, "You're close, but you left a little something off. The 'e' on the end." This was not merely an adult, but the Vice President of the United States, so William dutifully complied, and completed the word per the Vice President's instructions:

"P-O-T-A-T-O-E." But William had indeed been correct on his first try. He knew how to spell "potato," while the Vice President of the United States did not.

The media recorded the incident, and the damage was only beginning. William gave an interview to the *Trentonian* newspaper, where he said there might be some truth in many of the whispers he'd heard about the Vice President being "an idiot." The boy later appeared on *Late Night with David Letterman*, where he said of Vice President Quayle, "I know he's not an idiot, but he needs to study more. Do you have to go to college to be Vice President?"

It was indeed a bench-clearing pile-on—arguably beyond the bounds of fairness, but a perfect storm of disastrous and irresistible bad publicity nonetheless. Quayle attempted to calm the uproar with some good-natured self-deprecation. "I should have caught the mistake on that spelling bee card. But as Mark Twain once said, 'You should never trust a man who has only one way to spell a word.'"

He was attempting to be a good sport about the debacle, and that may have sufficed, except that the quote Quayle cited was from President Andrew Jackson, and not Mark Twain. But Quayle gamely tried to take the blame for that unfortunate error as well. "I should have remembered that was Andrew Jackson who said that, since he got his nickname 'Stonewall' by vetoing bills passed by Congress." Well-intentioned again—except that "Stonewall" Jackson was not President Andrew, but Confederate General Thomas J. "Stonewall" Jackson, who had in fact received his nickname after the first Battle of Bull Run.

FREE SPEACH

A persuasive argument could be made that only three people in U.S. history are as unfortunately quotable as Dan Quayle, and two of them are named George Bush. Esteemed company, yes, but Mr. Quayle very much holds his own. Quayle's gaffes, malapropisms, and downright butchering of the English language were legion during his term in office. On the campaign trail he attempted to show his grasp of the World War II genocide of the Jews by explaining, "The Holocaust was an obscene period in our nation's history. I mean in this century's history. But we all lived in this century. I didn't live in this century."

His first summer in office, he commemorated the 20th anniversary of the Apollo 11 moon landing, opening his remarks with "Welcome to President Bush, Mrs. Bush, and my fellow astronauts." Space was a big theme for Quayle that summer, and he continued to show the depth and breadth of his celestial awareness that September, when he said of the National Aeronautics and Space Agency, "For NASA, space is still a very high priority."

To his credit, he was always inquisitive. On a tour of a Manhattan AIDS clinic, apparently aware of the new retroviral drug being used to treat AIDS patients and prevent HIV, he asked the clinic director of the clinic's patients, "Are they taking DDT?"

Dan Quayle's finest oratory moment of his Vice Presidency, though, came on May 9, 1989, during a speech to the United Ne-

Fun Facts

Mere months after the famous exchange at the Quayle-Bentsen Vice Presidential debate, diners at Chinese restaurants in Portland, Oregon, and other cities reported receiving fortune cookies which produced the message, "You're no Jack Kennedy."

When, during the 1988 campaign, questions resurfaced about whether Dan Quayle had committed adultery with farm insurance lobbyist Paula Parkinson during an infamous Congressional golf junket in 1980, Marilyn Quayle defended her husband as only a loving and devoted wife could. "Anyone who knows Dan Quayle knows he would rather play golf than have sex any day."

gro College Fund, when he attempted to ingratiate himself with his audience by taking that one-of-a-kind Quayle cleaver to the group's venerable and universally known motto. "What a waste it is to lose one's mind. Or not to have a mind is being very wasteful. How true that is." Whatever else Quayle's contribution to American history, this has to be his crowning achievement, as it has earned inclusion in the esteemed *Bartlett's Familiar Quotations.*

BENTSEN BURNER

There had been murmurs throughout the campaign that George Bush had picked Dan Quayle in a cynical and ultimately misguided effort to tap the youth and charisma of John Fitzgerald Kennedy. If Bush's team was at all game to go along with this strategy, that had to end the moment that Dan Quayle opened his mouth in New Orleans, yet Quayle continued to invoke the comparison all along the hustings in Fall 1988. In their single Vice Presidential debate on October 5, one of the moderators, NBC's Tom Brokaw, broached the subject of Quayle's experiential fitness to assume the Presidency if necessary. With Pavlovian predictability, Quayle noted that, if asked to serve tomorrow, "I have as much experience in the Congress as Jack Kennedy did when he sought the Presidency."

What happened next was practically in slow motion to the millions of viewers watching across the country. As Judy Woodruff cued Quayle's opponent, Senator Lloyd Bentsen, for his reply, Bentsen merely smiled for the shortest moment, clearly thanking the Debate Gods for handing him this most golden of opportunities. Bentsen calmly placed the ball on the tee, licked a finger to confirm the windless conditions on the course, and confidently reared back and hit a monster across the fairway and onto the next green, bouncing into the cup for an ace. "Senator, I served with Jack Kennedy: I knew Jack Kennedy; Jack Kennedy was a friend of mine. Senator, you're no Jack Kennedy."

ALBERT GORE
DEMOCRAT, TENNESSEE
WITH BILL CLINTON, 1993–2001

To chroniclers of Vice Presidential ignominy, 1992 was a dispiriting return to the dark days of the mundane—the stultifying, sensible, steadfast, competence-run-amok of the Theodore Roosevelts and the Walter Mondales and the Thomas Riley Marshalls. This was an especially hard punch to the solar plexus after the wildly quotable and oratorically dizzying twelve years of Dan Quayle and George Herbert Walker Bush. Albert Gore was not a man who had only read newspapers or was the scion of people who owned them. He had actually written for them. He could complete his sentences with proper King's English and deliver them with cogent thoughts at their foundation. He couldn't have been any different from his predecessor. For one man, Harvard was his alma mater; for the other, it was likely little more than just another city in New England.

Like his predecessor, however, Albert Gore, Jr. came from hearty and well-to-do stock. His father, Albert, Sr., was a former Tennessee

*"The nation has watched Mr. Gore in a private search for his
public persona, or maybe a public search for a private persona;
by now it's hard to tell which."*
—The Washington Post

Congressman, Senator, and associate of FDR's Secretary of State,
Cordell Hull. His mother was only the second woman to graduate
from Vanderbilt University Law School.

Gore was an unlikely candidate for the Vice Presidency in 1992.
He had modest success at a run for the Presidential nomination in
1988 and seemed poised for a stronger run the next cycle, but removed
himself from the race after his young son was seriously injured in an
accident in 1989. Come the 1992 Democratic convention, Gore's son
was recovered and Clinton had the party's nomination in hand, giving
him the confidence to select a running mate equal to him in capability
and intellect. Gore saw in a Clinton Presidency an opportunity to do
more than warm a chair in the West Wing and fill in for the President
at boring events of state.

After eight tumultuous but ultimately peaceful and prosperous
years of Clinton's Presidency, Gore seemed in pole position to take
the top job himself in 2000, yet through a number of misjudgments
he managed to damage his campaign to the point of an election-night
mess with a far less qualified and intellectually rigorous opponent.
After more than a month of tedious and agonizing recounts and court
fights, Gore was ultimately the loser in one of the most controversial
elections in U.S. history. Despite winning the popular vote by more
than 500,000, the electoral results and ultimately the Presidency hinged
on the final count in Florida, a disaster beset by allegations of fraud
and fierce partisan wrangling in state courts, legislatures, and—some
accuse—the Supreme Court. It is reasonably pointed out, though, that
if Gore had merely carried his home state of Tennessee, the issue would
have been moot, and the only reasons people would remember Florida
today would be for the Space Shuttle, Disney World, and 80-year-olds
who drive for miles with their left turn signal on.

Gore would enjoy an unusual resurgence in popularity in 2006 with his filmed global warming discussion, *An Inconvenient Truth*, which won him an Academy Award. The documentary influenced a number of politicians and industry leaders who had heretofore turned a deaf ear to environmental concerns, among them former Chrysler chief Lee Iacocca, who told NPR that it was Gore's "Power Point presentation" that had almost single-handedly changed his opinion about the sustainability of fossil fuels.

...AND THUS REINVENTED PORNOGRAPHY

During a March 9, 1999 interview with CNN's Wolf Blitzer, Vice President Gore said in an interview, "During my service in the United States Congress, I took the initiative in creating the Internet," explaining that throughout his time in Congress he continually pushed for funding research grants and other investment in developing the technology that would ultimately develop the World Wide Web. This comment was famously twisted and taken out of context, and Gore was ridiculed throughout the next election cycle and beyond as having claimed to have "invented the Internet." This was just one of several comments that were twisted by the Republican opposition to make Gore appear to have delusions of grandeur and to be a wild-eyed utopian out of touch with reality. Such opposition tactics, as well as Gore's insistence upon distancing himself from his popular boss and predecessor, Bill Clinton, only contributed to Gore's defeat in 2000.

Fun Facts

As a freshman at Harvard, Gore's roommate was future actor Tommy Lee Jones.

Reclusive and reportedly bitter after his 2000 defeat, Gore was lampooned in the *Onion* as delivering an imaginary address to the nation in front of his bathroom mirror after the 9/11 attacks, and holding a cabinet meeting at his dining room table with his two cats.

TIPPER AND SUE AND (DEE) SNIDER TOO

Despite his solid Democratic bona fides, Al Gore was never a darling of the American Left, for little other reason than the shrill crusade against "offensive" rock lyrics that was launched by his wife, Tipper; Reagan Treasury Secretary James Baker's wife, Susan; and a coterie of other "Washington wives" who were terrified that their children were being brainwashed by universally available rock lyrics into becoming whores, baby-killers, rapists, and suicide casualties. The red flag that enraged Tipper came in 1984, when she discovered her young daughter, Karenna, listening to one of Prince's more tedious and banal "sexxxxed-up" tracks, "Darling Nikki."

With an alacrity only possible with their husbands' legislative and administrative connections, the Parents' Musical Resource Committee, or PMRC, formed in May 1985. By August of that year it had pressured 19 record labels into placing "Parental Guidance: Explicit Lyrics" on certain albums, and in September, with a posse of notoriously stodgy and scolding Senators at their side, it went head-to-head on Capitol Hill with labeling opponents Frank Zappa, Dee Snider of Twisted Sister, and John Denver, who noted the absurdity of music censorship by telling of the outraged folks inflamed by his "controversial," sleep-inducing acoustic ballad, "Rocky Mountain High." The stickers went on, but the profanity continued and even escalated.

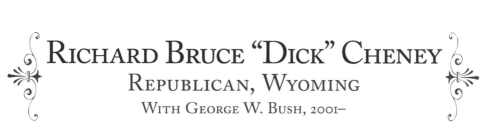

RICHARD BRUCE "DICK" CHENEY
REPUBLICAN, WYOMING
WITH GEORGE W. BUSH, 2001–

Prior to 2001, not many people would have found the Face of Evil in a grumpy, balding, ex-Congressman from Wyoming, but it didn't take long after George W. Bush's election in 2000 for Vice President Dick Cheney to become Voldemort in the eyes of many of his detractors. With his icy, silent glares and his snarling denunciations of the media and his political opponents, Cheney exudes the palpable, if unfounded, sense that he has either killed men with his bare hands or hired shadowy others to do it for him in Washington D.C. parking garages very late at night.

Given the reputation that has accompanied him to a job approval rating of as low as 18%, it's perhaps fitting that Cheney's tentacles in Washington extend back to before the Watergate Era, as a White House staff assistant to President Nixon. Nixon's successor, Gerald Ford, would make Dick Cheney his White House Chief of Staff.

As a Congressman in the 1980s, Cheney distinguished himself with right-of-mainstream stands such as voting against a holiday for Martin Luther King, Jr., and nay on imposing sanctions on the pro-apartheid government of South Africa.

The history of the last twenty years would likely have been far different if it weren't for the drinking, extramarital affairs, and unseemly relationships with defense contractors of former Texas Senator John Tower, President George H. W. Bush's first nominee for Secretary of Defense. After Bush's brutal campaign against Michael Dukakis in 1988, the Democratic Congress may also have had some measure of revenge on their mind in rejecting Tower, sending him from nominee to ignominy. In any case, Dick Cheney had been poised to take a leadership role in his party following his latest re-election to the House in 1988. With Tower's emphatic rejection, though, Bush called on Cheney to be his new Secretary of Defense, and the man from Wyoming surrendered a powerful future in Congress as Minority Whip to a junior bomb-thrower by the name of Newt Gingrich.

Cheney still got to partake of some excitement in his new job: He was Bush's number one man at the Pentagon during the collapse of the Soviet Bloc and Operation Desert Storm. It was a jolt when his boss lost his job in 1992 to those two Hippies, Clinton and Gore.

"Go fuck yourself."
—Vice President Cheney on the Senate floor, to Vermont
Senator Patrick Leahy, in what is apparently
a traditional Wyoming greeting.

Suddenly out of work himself, Cheney spent a brief sojourn at one of those seemingly ubiquitous think tanks hording all of America's well-connected former politicians angling for a high-paying job that only requires their attendance seven or eight hours every three months. But presiding over the New World Order and helping call the plays for America's triumphant return to overseas war had been big work and pretty heady stuff, and Cheney even considered a run for the White House in 1996.

In the end, he opted for a position with engineering and construction giant Haliburton. And there he likely would have stayed, just another harrumphing Caucasian male with a bad heart holding a no-heavy-lifting job in a petroleum-related industry—until 2000 when the elder Bush came calling again.

Cheney was tapped to head up Bush son George W.'s Vice Presidential Selection Committee. Dad called out all of his old friends to help his somewhat dimmer, less ambitious son reclaim the keys to the old family bungalow. Dick Cheney had been loyal, hardworking, and had always shown impeccable judgment. So it was no surprise when Cheney rejected all the old GOP luminaries who might make young George look bad, as well as the promising, but somewhat flaccid, bright young hopes of the party who would be formidable powers in their own right someday, but in the meantime would leave the ticket more than a few pounds short of a welter-weight qualifying bout. There was only one man who could keep hold of the reins of government and quietly pull all the switches behind the curtain lest anyone think the boy was actually running the country himself; a man powerful enough to steer the ship of state, but who didn't have the ego to need credit for it—someone for whom his stock options and the fringe benefits of Vice Presidential glad-handing would be reward enough (well, that, and maybe the occasional piece of an oil drilling contract in a caribou reserve to pay for an Aspen condo for his daughter).

But who? Colin Powell was a perennial "no" just as emphatically as he was when asked if he would consider a Presidential bid, and was quickly gaining a reputation as the GOP's Mario Cuomo. John Danforth didn't want it. John McCain would bring the voters, but the former Vietnam POW was an almost-certain ticking time bomb given the character-bludgeoning that Bush's people laid on him in South Carolina after McCain destroyed Bush in the New Hampshire primary. Actor and former Tennessee Senator Fred Thompson was on the short list, but he still had the stink of *Curly Sue* and *Aces: Iron Eagle III* on him, and that might cost them a few of the "intellectual" states. Jack Kemp still had both JFK hair and major supply-sider street cred, but had done nothing for the ticket in '96. And God love elder statesman Bob Dole, but he was shilling for Viagra and was late for a life of windbreakers and metal detectors on the sands of Boca Raton.

There was only one man who could do the job: The man from Wyoming, Richard Bruce Cheney.

YOU BETTER BE SORRY

Always the rugged sportsman, Vice President Cheney and a group of friends embarked on a hunting excursion in the wilds of Texas hunting country in February 2006. Some clarification is in order, though: the "excursion" was conducted from a small convoy of luxury vehicles, the "Texas hunting country" was a posh private ranch, and the "hunting" involved pen-raised pheasants kept in cages until the hunters arrived and got out of their cars, at which point the birds were released into the "wilds" (or as the Senior Vice President of the Human Society less charitably characterized it, "an open-air abattoir") where they stood a roughly 17% chance of eluding their blue-blooded, often-geriatric pursuers.

On Saturday, February 11, 2006, Cheney and his party got out of their town cars to pursue a newly liberated bevy of quail, lest they make it back to their secure-enclosure habitat and tell the others what

was in store for them. The Vice President, armed with his Perazzi 28-gauge shotgun, was stalking his deliberately challenged prey. Meanwhile, the VP's friend, Austin lawyer Harry Whittington, 78, had fallen behind the party as he ran back to recover his own kill. He was approaching Cheney from behind when the covey flushed, and the Vice President turned and fired, shooting Whittington in the face—or as ranch owner Katharine Armstrong would more breezily describe it, "peppered (him) pretty good."

As a result of that "peppering"—which wasn't disclosed to the media for a day—Whittington was in intensive care, and he suffered a minor heart attack when subcutaneous birdshot moved and lodged in his heart. He recovered and was released from the hospital after seven days. The Vice President assumed full responsibility for the shooting, and it was officially categorized and dismissed as an accident.

As a testament to either Whittington's magnanimity or the Vice President's *Manchurian Candidate*-like hypnotic prowess, Whittington would later issue an apology to the Vice President for the stress that the shooting has caused him.

BOSS KILLA

Depending on how the rest of his term plays out, George W. Bush will be the first U.S. President to hire Dick Cheney and not suddenly face an early retirement. Cheney's first job in the Nixon White House came in 1969, where he served a number of positions before Nixon resigned under pressure and disgrace in 1974. As Chief of Staff for Nixon's successor, Gerald Ford, Cheney presided over a number of questionable moves—including the sacking of larger-than-life Henry Kissinger—and encouraged Ford to dump the more liberal Nelson Rockefeller from the 1976 ticket in favor of the slightly less warm and engaging Bob Dole, a move widely credited with tipping a close election, and what Ford would go on to call "the biggest political mistake of my life." Ronald Reagan had the good sense not to hire Cheney and served his two terms. George H.W. Bush, however, hired Cheney, where he began to form the neo-conservative positions he currently

Fun Facts

Dick Cheney appeared in 1995's *Die Hard With A Vengeance*. He plays the other scowling, bald policeman.

When traveling, Vice President Cheney demands that his hotel suites be set at a comfortable 68 degrees; offer four cans of Diet Sprite (caffeine-free—the old ticker, you know!); provide for his wife, Lynne, two bottles of Calistoga or Perrier (as The Smoking Gun website calls it, "a favored beverage of French terrorism appeasers"); and have all televisions preset to Fox News Channel.

In 2003, Cheney, joined by friends, including ex-Dallas Cowboys quarterback Roger Staubach and Texas Senator John Cornyn, visited Rolling Rock Ranch in Liognier Township, Pennsylvania. On the day of their arrival, some 500 farm-raised pheasants were released for the hunting pleasure of the Vice President and his companions. Together they managed to bag 417 of the survival-challenged birds, or 83.4%. The odds of survival for the pen-raised birds were especially dismal when they were pursued by the Vice President, who managed to bag 70 of them himself.

espouses today for Bush's son. By the end of the first George H.W. Bush administration, Cheney and his core of adherents within the administration were "referred to collectively as 'the crazies,'" according to Ray McGovern, a CIA intelligence specialist who has worked for Presidents back to JFK. And the first George H.W. Bush administration was the only George H.W. Bush administration. When George W. Bush won election to the Presidency in 2000, his father's most trusted advisers, Secretary of State James Baker and National Security Adviser Brent Scowcroft, told the younger Bush of Cheney and his proteges, "Keep these guys at arm's length." Bush didn't listen, but at least he's been able to keep his job. So far.

WHICH CAME FIRST—THE CHICKENHAWK OR THE EGG?

Though you wouldn't know it by his unwavering hawkish stance or by his willingness to send other people's children to do America's bidding in foreign lands, Dick Cheney was not above employing some creative measures to avoid the draft. He was neither the first nor the most prominent of his generation to finagle to avoid being drafted into military service during Vietnam, but he certainly deserves mention for the considerable lengths to which he went to keep himself stateside. While certainly intelligent, Cheney never displayed much interest in improving himself through education. Still, the U.S. presence in Vietnam began to escalate under Lyndon Johnson. Having already left Yale and taken a job with a telephone company repair crew, Cheney signed up for courses at Casper Community College and then went on to the University of Wyoming (apparently there weren't any available military deferments for utility linemen from Wyoming).

On August 7th, 1964, following the Gulf of Tonkin incident, Congress voted to accelerate U.S. involvement in Vietnam. Now it wasn't enough to be a student to avoid the draft. So Cheney married his high school girlfriend, Lynne Vincent. That bought him time until October 26th of the following year, when deferment rules were tightened again. Then Lynne Cheney gave birth to the couple's first daughter, Elizabeth—exactly nine months and two days after the Selective Service changed the deferment rules to render married men eligible for conscription unless, of course, they had children. This was just another of five deferments that Cheney received throughout the war. "I had other priorities in the '60s than military service," Cheney would tell the *Washington Post* in 1989, echoing the sentiments of other anti-authoritarian rabble-rousers of his era.

Third-Party Candidates
& Notable Also-Rans

General Curtis LeMay
American Independent Party
With George Wallace, 1968

The 1968 candidacy of George Wallace was not what one might call a kinder, gentler, big-tent kind of campaign. This was the man, after all, who promised to run over any demonstrator who got in the way of his limo; who told protesters "I was killing fascists when you punks were in diapers"; who ran against welfare and the Civil Rights Act of 1964; and whose rallying cry, "Segregation now, segregation tomorrow, segregation forever!" was written for him by a Ku Klux Klansman that he hired as a speechwriter.

After a strong run at the Presidency in 1964 as a Democrat, Wallace ran in 1968 as the first candidate of the American Independent Party. For his running mate, Wallace selected a man in whose unit Wallace had served as a sergeant in World War II—retired U.S. Air Force General Curtis LeMay. LeMay—also known by his nickname "Bombs Away"—was already famous for his clashes with Robert McNamara and other members of the Kennedy and Johnson Administrations whom he felt weren't sufficiently proactive in addressing American military matters. In fact, it was General LeMay who first coined the swaggeringly American phrase "bomb them back into the Stone Age."

Wallace was a Southern governor and needed to balance his ticket with strength in military and foreign policy. And boy, did he get it and then some with Curtis LeMay. The General made his name in World War II, overhauling the air war against Japan by abandoning targeted daytime bombings in favor of a night-after-night-after-night firebombing of the country, leading to the obliteration of 63 Japanese cities and a half-million people. LeMay was circumspect about his war command. "Killing Japanese didn't bother me very much at that time…I suppose if I had lost the war, I would have been tried as a war criminal."

The General kicked off his campaign with Wallace by criticizing the conventional "phobia" about using nuclear weapons. If atomic and hydrogen bombs were really all that bad, he wondered, then how come life was so triumphantly returning to the Bikini Atoll, the Micronesian island that America test-bombed into the Stone Age in the 1940s and 50s?

As political reporter Jules Witcover tells the story, LeMay's coming out can only be imagined as a Presidential nominee's worst nightmare. Of the Atoll, LeMay noted that "everything is about the same except the land crabs," which, he conceded, were still "a little bit hot." Oh, but the rats, though! The rats on the island were "bigger, fatter and healthier than they ever were before." On the topic of nuclear warfare, LeMay speculated that there wasn't much difference between being killed by a nuclear weapon and a rusty knife. In fact, if he had his druthers, LeMay said he'd rather be killed by a nuke.

As reporter Dan Carter noted of the mortified Governor, "For once in his life, George Wallace was speechless."

Wallace had hoped to capture enough electoral votes to prevent a majority and throw the election into the House of Representatives. They fell short, but he and LeMay captured four states and 46 electoral votes.

There are probably hundreds of thousands of pages of mythology devoted to tales of Wendigo, Gorgons, Minotaurs, and Perytons, but unlike the dubious and unsubstantiated accounts of these ravenous and terrifying monsters, we have incontrovertible proof that there once walked on this Earth voting-age men and women who chose to put General Curtis LeMay a heartbeat away from the most powerful office in the free world.

Thomas Eagleton
Democrat, Missouri
With George S. McGovern, 1972

The cadre of grizzled party vets and their army of young, smart, hungry, mean-business campaign worker bees pulled off an amazing feat landing the 1972 Democratic nomination for anti-war Senator George S. McGovern. McGovern entered the campaign season just one of eleven candidates who weren't Ted Kennedy, who'd been the party's hope for unseating Nixon until he took the bridge too far at Chappaquiddick in 1969.

The clear favorite after Kennedy was Maine Senator and Hubert Humphrey's 1968 running mate, Ed Muskie. Nixon's crew worried that, of all the eleven Democratic aspirants, Muskie had a plausible shot of unseating the President. The Committee to Re-Elect the President (CREEP) created and leaked to the *Manchester Union Leader* a forged letter known to infamy as "the Canuck letter," which appeared to portray Muskie speaking pejoratively of French-Canadians residing in America. In his zeal to repudiate the letter, Muskie melted down in spectacular fashion, in his now famous "crying speech" in front of the paper's offices. According to news accounts at the time, the Senator had "broken down three times in as many minutes" and he was "weeping silently." Muskie feebly defended himself that if his voice cracked, it was out of anger, and that what appeared to be tears was actually melted snow on his face. But there's no crying in Presidential politics. It was an abject humiliation, top-to-bottom, and the Man from Maine was through.

"The McGovern Army" stepped into the maw and secured enough delegates for their man to take the nomination in Miami after a frenzied, last-minute delegate fight at the convention. All they had to do now was choose a running mate, and then they could devote their energies to beating Nixon in the fall. Unfortunately, they got ahead of themselves, and none of the diligence and fanatical attention to every detail that got them the nomination was in evidence in choosing said running mate.

McGovern believed all along that Ted Kennedy would agree to be his running mate if he won the nomination. Advisers who were close to the next great hope of the Kennedy clan insisted to McGovern again and again that Teddy wasn't interested. "Within two years," said a Kennedy friend, "Vice President Kennedy would be a sad-eyed, overweight drunk." Certainly, it's American history's good fortune that he stayed in the Senate and avoided that ignominious fate.

Starting with a list of over 50 names, McGovern was rebuffed by Senators Walter Mondale, Abraham Ribicoff, and Gaylord Nelson; Florida Governor Reuben Askew; and United Auto Workers President Leonard Woodcock. Continuing down the list, McGovern considered Boston Mayor Kevin White, but found that he'd be facing a boycott from the Massachusetts delegation because of White's earlier support for Muskie. McGovern himself said he would have chosen Muskie had it not been for the last-minute delegate fight.

The candidate's short list was empty, except for one name: Senator Thomas Eagleton of Missouri. Young, bright, charismatic, a natural campaigner from a border state, and an eager and enthusiastic albatross ready and available to weigh down the party and destroy their already slim chances of beating Richard Nixon in 1972.

SHOCK THE DONKEY

Eagleton was almost too enthusiastic about taking the position, and that should have been their first red flag. He had been going around the convention the previous few days announcing that he was "ecstatically available." When Senator McGovern—having exhausted all his other possibilities—finally called, Eagleton said, "George, before you change your mind, I accept."

And that was that. Eagleton would give his acceptance speech, McGovern would give his the next night, and then it was off on the campaign trail to make Nixon a one-term aberration.

It's not known how the question was posed to him, but given the fiasco that ensued, one wonders if Eagleton assumed McGovern's people were being literal when asking him if he had any skeletons in his closet, as he confidently answered in the negative.

That was the extent of their background check.

They shouldn't have been surprised, then, when reports began to circulate that Eagleton had been hospitalized several times for psychiatric care in the 1960s, including two administrations of electro-shock therapy.

For all the unflattering and undignified situations that America's past Vice Presidents had found themselves in, the thought of the nation's leader-in-reserve being strapped to a table and having electrodes applied to his temples like a scene out of Shock Corridor was apparently more than a little off-putting—if not necessarily to the American electorate, then at least to the man who nominated him.

McGovern at first said that he was standing by his nominee "1000 percent." But with every newspaper editorial and new twist on the story, McGovern's position migrated all over the map. Worse, he appeared to be letting the matter play itself out in the press, which is where Eagleton seemed to be getting much of his information on where his nomination stood.

All told, McGovern handled the revelations badly, and his vacillation, maneuvering, and indecision were to many a very telling portent of what America could expect from a President McGovern. The Eagleton affair was the beginning of the end of the McGovern candidacy. McGovern dumped Tom Eagleton for Kennedy brother-in-law Sargent Shriver. In November, the two were beaten by over 18 million votes, losing every electoral vote except 14 from Massachusetts and 3 from the District of Columbia. Eagleton would acknowledge his own role as being "one rock in a landslide."

REP. GERALDINE FERRARO
DEMOCRAT, NEW YORK
WITH WALTER MONDALE, 1984

Walter Mondale faced a daunting task in 1984 going up against popular incumbent President Ronald Reagan. The Reagan team was salivating over going to war with the liberal Minnesotan and former Vice President after Mondale upended the two candidates they feared would be much more formidable, Ohio Senator John Glenn and Colorado Senator Gary Hart. In Mondale's mind, a bold move was in order to set off the campaign with a boom—and radioactive Jesse Jackson wasn't the other half of the ticket (fresh off his "Hymietown" remark about New York City, his selection would surely have done a number on the Jewish vote).

The Veep Short List has become a quadrennial dog-and-pony show, and Walter Mondale made the most of his moment as Best In Show Judge. Around the circle came African-American Mayors Tom Bradley of Los Angeles and Wilson Goode of Philadelphia, San Francisco Mayor Dianne Feinstein, Kentucky Governor Martha Layne Collins, and Senator Lloyd Bentsen of Texas with its 29 electoral votes.

Mondale selected Ferraro, a three-term Congresswoman from working-class Queens, New York, because she personified middle class and could help with blue-collar voters. The choice was a big hit among the party faithful, but did little to bridge the gender gap with Ronald Reagan. A CBS News/*New York Times* poll taken shortly after the selection revealed that 60% of respondents thought of the Ferraro selection as a sop to feminist groups who had been bringing pressure on Mondale to choose a woman.

The choice united the convention, but that was as good as it got for the Democrats that year. Mondale believed that the voters wanted candor and inexplicably used his acceptance speech to announce that, "Mr. Reagan will raise your taxes, and so will I. The difference is that he won't tell you, and I just did." That's not the kind of candor that wins votes.

Their campaign wasn't helped by her refusal to release business and tax information about her husband, John Zaccaro. Rumors swirled about connections to organized crime, and that he'd raided a trust fund that he was overseeing. In the end, it was disclosed that he was renting property to a company that distributed pornographic films and a Chinese sweat shop, and that he owed a considerable amount in back taxes, but was paying it back.

The campaign was sunk anyway, and Mondale and Ferraro were shellacked, forty-nine states to one, carrying only Mondale's home state of Minnesota, and the District of Columbia.

WHAT RHYMES WITH "HATERIARCH"?

Ferraro was going head-to-head with Vice President George Bush, and there was no love lost between Congresswoman Ferraro and the Second Lady and matriarch of the Bush Family, Barbara Bush. Mondale and Ferraro assailed the Bushes as wealthy society creatures who were out of touch with ordinary, working-class people. When asked to comment on Air Force Two while returning from a Columbus Day parade in New York, Mrs. Bush snapped to reporters that Ferraro and her husband had more money than the Bushes and called the Vice Presidential candidate "a four-million-dollar…I can't say it but it rhymes with rich." She later called Ferraro to apologize for suggesting she was a "witch," but nearly a quarter-century later a skeptic or two still think that she may have had another word in mind.

OFF TO THE RACES

Ferraro made a splash in 2008 as a member of the finance committee for the Hillary Clinton Presidential Campaign when she popped a vein and went after the press for giving the Senator Barack Obama campaign what she thought was a free pass. She suggested that his wildly popular candidacy was the result of some form of electoral affirmative action. "If Obama was a white man, he would not be in this position. And if he was a woman (of any color) he would not be in this position. He happens to be very lucky to be who he is. And the country is caught up in the concept."

As that March week wore on and the ire over Ferraro's remarks rose, Ferraro kept digging. "Racism works in two different directions. I really think they're attacking me because I'm white. How's that?"

The Clinton campaign issued a tepid repudiation of her comments and the debate continues whether Ferraro was a loose cannon, or whether she sacrificed herself with the tacit approval of the campaign to force the press to more deeply scrutinize Senator Obama.

Suspicion of her racial motivations deepened when it was revealed that she had made similar comments in 1988 when party establishment favorite Michael Dukakis was in the middle of a heated primary battle with Reverend Jesse Jackson. With that, many decided that Ms. Ferraro both walked like a duck and talked like a duck, and drew their own conclusions accordingly.

Ferraro was defiant in the response to her outburst, deploying her own brand of Queens logic that said the Obama campaign actually owed *her* an apology. With that, former Congressman Ferraro flashed an angry middle finger behind her and walked away from Hillary's team.

Admiral James Stockdale
Independent
With H. Ross Perot

George Herbert Walker Bush came out of the first Gulf War practically bulletproof, with approval ratings hovering around 90%. The unpalatable thought of desperately trying to raise the necessary millions only to be shellacked by the Bush-Quayle Re-election Juggernaut was daunting enough to keep most marquee Democrats out of the race, including New York Governor Mario Cuomo and Georgia Senator Sam Nunn. Limping into 1992, the Dems were stuck with an uninspiring lot that the media would dub "the Seven Dwarves."

By that time, though, the economy was stagnating and Bush's invincibility rating had evaporated. His war triumph was all but forgotten, and the GOP faithful had seized on him as if he were a bloodied herd animal for breaking his "read my lips—no new taxes!" pledge from 1988. But despite the disappointment of his party, he did have the advantage of incumbency, and except for a challenge on his right by Pat Buchanan, he had his re-nomination locked up. And, with the Democrats down to a Senator of dubious health, a far-left 70s political luminary known pejoratively as "Governor Moonbeam," and a smooth, glad-handing Arkansan whom most people were loathe to trust around their daughters much less their country, the American electorate appeared prepared to hold their noses and re-elect the President for another four years.

Then on February 20, 1992, enigmatic Texas billionaire H. Ross Perot appeared on *Larry King Live* and declared his independent candidacy for President if his supporters could get his name on the ballot in all 50 States. Thus began one of the strangest and most mercurial romances in American political history. Tired of politicians as usual, the country was charmed by Perot's homespun humor and auto-repair metaphors. Sober, serious men of politics from both sides of the aisle like Ed Rollins and Hamilton Jordan pledged themselves to his campaign.

Long an outspoken supporter of Vietnam Veterans, POWs, and MIAs, Perot immediately selected former POW and 26-time-decorated Vietnam Vet, Admiral James Stockdale, to be a "placeholder" on his ticket until a permanent running mate could be formally named. Stockdale's story was both harrowing and fascinating (he mutilated himself and beat himself bloody with a chair to prevent his captors from using him for propaganda footage), but it was lost in the din of the campaign—and in his disastrous appearance in the Vice Presidential debate.

Stockdale hadn't planned to still be on the ticket, let alone participate in a nationally televised debate. Perot's petulance and prickliness bubbled to the surface as the campaign wore on, and by July—after he accused GOP tacticians of attempting to sabotage his daughter's wedding—he briefly bowed out of the race. He had a change of heart come fall, and by the time the Vice Presidential debate rolled around, Stockdale was informed he would be participating and had less than a week to prepare.

He began the debate by asking, "Who am I? Why am I here?" It was apparently intended to be rhetorical and to allow him to share his life story—that he was in the same flight class as John Glenn, was present at the second Gulf of Tonkin "attack" (which he confirmed wasn't an attack at all), and had served seven years as a POW.

Unfortunately, the debate continued and he didn't have the chance to elaborate, and for the rest of the evening appeared confused and not in possession of all his faculties (at one point, he asked moderator Hal Bruno to repeat a question because "I didn't have my hearing aid turned up"). It's unfortunate that Stockdale didn't hit his stride that evening: While Gore's military credentials were relatively solid, if no match for the Admiral's, Stockdale could easily have turned Dan Quayle's privileged maneuverings around Vietnam service into another humiliating snare much like Senator Lloyd Bentsen's devastating "you're no Jack Kennedy."

Stockdale's presence on the ticket was mystifying for one other reason that had nothing to do with his mental fitness: Long accustomed to doing things his own way, Perot apparently had little or no use for a Vice President were he to be elected. Said Stockdale, "I never had a single conversation about politics with Ross Perot in my life; still haven't."

Perot and Stockdale won nearly 19% of the popular vote in November, but no electoral votes. Theirs was the most successful third-party effort in a Presidential election since Teddy Roosevelt ran on the Bull Moose ticket in 1912.

BIBLIOGRAPHY

Chapter 1: John Adams
Tally, Steve, *Bland Ambition*, Orlando, Harcourt Brace Jovanovich, 1992, pp 1-9
Barzman, Sol, *Madmen and Geniuses*, Chicago, Follett, 1974, pp 14-19
Witcover, Jules, *Crapshoot: Rolling the Dice on the Vice Presidency*, New York, Crown, 1992
Vice Presidents: A Biographical Dictionary, New York, Checkmark Books, 2001, L. Edward Purcell, editor;
     by Jack D. Warren, 1-13
http://en.wikipedia.org/wiki/John_Adams#Vice_Presidency
http://www.claremont.org/publications/crb/id.849/article_detail.asp
http://bioguide.congress.gov/scripts/biodisplay.pl?index=I000053
http://www.doctorzebra.com/prez/g02.htm
http://en.wikipedia.org/wiki/John_Adams
Beyer, Rick, *The Greatest Presidential Stories Never Told*, New York, Collins, 2007

Chapter 2: Thomas Jefferson
Tally, Steve, *Bland Ambition*, Orlando, Harcourt Brace Jovanovich, 1992, pp 10-19
Barzman, Sol, *Madmen and Geniuses*, Chicago, Follett, 1974, pp 20-25
Witcover, Jules, *Crapshoot: Rolling the Dice on the Vice Presidency*, New York, Crown, 1992
Vice Presidents: A Biographical Dictionary, New York, Checkmark Books, 2001, L. Edward Purcell, editor;
     by Eugene R. Sheridan, pp 14-21
http://www.twbookmark.com/books/42/0316082678/chapter_excerpt10835.html
http://www.archives.gov/education/lessons/electoral-tally/
http://en.wikipedia.org/wiki/Burr-Hamilton_duel
http://www.senate.gov/artandhistory/history/common/generic/VP_Thomas_Jefferson.htm
http://www.constitutionfacts.com/Founding_Fathers/FascinatingFF.htm
http://www.pbs.org/newshour/inauguration/history.htm
http://www.thenation.com/blogs/thebeat?pid=2135
Beyer, Rick, *The Greatest Presidential Stories Never Told*, New York, Collins, 2007

Chapter 3: Aaron Burr
Tally, Steve, *Bland Ambition*, Orlando, Harcourt Brace Jovanovich, 1992, pp 20-31
Barzman, Sol, *Madmen and Geniuses*, Chicago, Follett, 1974, pp 26-33
Witcover, Jules, *Crapshoot: Rolling the Dice on the Vice Presidency*, New York, Crown, 1992
Vice Presidents: A Biographical Dictionary, New York, Checkmark Books, 2001, L. Edward Purcell, editor;
     by Mary-Jo Kline, pp 23-31
Harwood, Michael, *In the Shadow of Presidents*, New York, J.B. Lippincott, 1966, pp 138-143
Chandler Waldrup, Carole, *The Vice Presidents*, Jefferson, NC, McFarland, 2006, pp 141-144
http://www.senate.gov/artandhistory/history/common/generic/VP_Aaron_Burr.htm
Beyer, Rick, *The Greatest Presidential Stories Never Told*, New York, Collins, 2007

Chapter 4: George Clinton
Tally, Steve, *Bland Ambition*, Orlando, Harcourt Brace Jovanovich, 1992, pp 35-40
Barzman, Sol, *Madmen and Geniuses*, Chicago, Follett, 1974, pp 34-39
Witcover, Jules, *Crapshoot: Rolling the Dice on the Vice Presidency*, New York, Crown, 1992

http://bioguide.congress.gov/scripts/biodisplay.pl?index=C000527
http://en.wikipedia.org/wiki/George_Clinton_%28vice_president%29

Chapter 5: Elbridge Gerry
Tally, Steve, *Bland Ambition*, Orlando, Harcourt Brace Jovanovich, 1992, pp 41-46
Barzman, Sol, *Madmen and Geniuses*, Chicago, Follett, 1974, pp 40-45
Witcover, Jules, *Crapshoot: Rolling the Dice on the Vice Presidency*, New York, Crown, 1992
http://bioguide.congress.gov/scripts/biodisplay.pl?index=C000527
http://en.wikipedia.org/wiki/George_Clinton_%28vice_president%29

Chapter 6: Daniel Tompkins
Tally, Steve, *Bland Ambition*, Orlando, Harcourt Brace Jovanovich, 1992, pp 47-52
Barzman, Sol, *Madmen and Geniuses*, Chicago, Follett, 1974, pp 40-45
Witcover, Jules, *Crapshoot: Rolling the Dice on the Vice Presidency*, New York, Crown, 1992
http://www.britannica.com/presidents/article-9072841
http://www.senate.gov/artandhistory/history/common/generic/VP_Daniel_Tompkins.htm
http://www.usatrivia.com/vpbitomp.html

Chapter 7: John C. Calhoun
Tally, Steve, *Bland Ambition*, Orlando, Harcourt Brace Jovanovich, 1992, pp 53-63
Barzman, Sol, *Madmen and Geniuses*, Chicago, Follett, 1974, pp 40-45
Witcover, Jules, *Crapshoot: Rolling the Dice on the Vice Presidency*, New York, Crown, 1992
http://en.wikipedia.org/wiki/John_c_calhoun
http://en.wikipedia.org/wiki/U.S._presidential_election%2C_1824
http://www.answers.com/topic/the-gorgeous-hussy-film

Chapter 8: Martin Van Buren
Tally, Steve, *Bland Ambition*, Orlando, Harcourt Brace Jovanovich, 1992, pp 53-70
Barzman, Sol, *Madmen and Geniuses*, Chicago, Follett, 1974, pp 52-65
Witcover, Jules, *Crapshoot: Rolling the Dice on the Vice Presidency*, New York, Crown, 1992
http://en.wikipedia.org/wiki/Martin_Van_Buren#Vice-Presidency
http://www.nndb.com/people/654/000026576/
http://www.mises.org/story/2201#ref1 ([1] As quoted in William Cabell Bruce, John
        Randolph of Roanoke, 1773 — 1833: A Biography Based Largely on New Material
        (New York: G.P Putnam's Sons, 1922), vol. 2, p. 203; and John Niven, Martin Van
        Buren: The Romantic Age of American Politics (New York: Oxford University Press,
        1983), p. 358.)
http://en.wikipedia.org/wiki/Angelica_Van_Buren
http://www.authorama.com/famous-affinities-of-history-ii-3.html
http://www.senate.gov/artandhistory/history/resources/pdf/VPTies.pdf

Chapter 9: Richard Mentor Johnson
Tally, Steve, *Bland Ambition*, Orlando, Harcourt Brace Jovanovich, 1992, pp 71-76
pp 60-65
Witcover, Jules, *Crapshoot: Rolling the Dice on the Vice Presidency*, New York, Crown, 1992
http://en.wikipedia.org/wiki/Martin_Van_Buren#Vice-Presidency
http://www.nndb.com/people/654/000026576/
http://www.mises.org/story/2201#ref1 ([1] As quoted in William Cabell Bruce, John
        Randolph of Roanoke, 1773 — 1833: A Biography Based Largely on New Material

(New York: G.P Putnam's Sons, 1922), vol. 2, p. 203; and John Niven, Martin Van Buren: The Romantic Age of American Politics (New York: Oxford University Press, 1983), p. 358.)
http://en.wikipedia.org/wiki/Angelica_Van_Buren
http://www.authorama.com/famous-affinities-of-history-ii-3.html

Chapter 10: John Tyler
Tally, Steve, *Bland Ambition*, Orlando, Harcourt Brace Jovanovich, 1992, pp 77-84
Barzman, Sol, *Madmen and Geniuses*, Chicago, Follett, 1974, pp 60-65
Witcover, Jules, *Crapshoot: Rolling the Dice on the Vice Presidency*, New York, Crown, 1992
http://en.wikipedia.org/wiki/Twenty-fifth_Amendment_to_the_United_States_
    Constitution#Text_of_the_Amendment
http://www.doctorzebra.com/prez/g10.htm
http://fs6.depauw.edu:50080/~jkochanczyk/president/tyler.html
http://home.att.net/~howingtons/tyler.html
http://www.loc.gov/rr/program/bib/ourdocs/Constitution.html
http://www.law.cornell.edu/constitution/constitution.articleii.html
http://www.whitehouse.gov/history/presidents/jt10.html
http://en.wikipedia.org/wiki/John_Tyler

Chapter 11: George Mifflin Dallas
Tally, Steve, *Bland Ambition*, Orlando, Harcourt Brace Jovanovich, 1992, pp 89-94
Barzman, Sol, *Madmen and Geniuses*, Chicago, Follett, 1974, pp 78-83
Vice Presidents: A Biographical Dictionary, New York, Checkmark Books, 2001, L. Edward Purcell, editor,
    by John M. Belohlavek, pp 102-112
http://en.wikipedia.org/wiki/Slogan
http://en.wikipedia.org/wiki/George_M._Dallas
http://www.senate.gov/artandhistory/history/common/generic/VP_George_Dallas.htm
http://freepages.history.rootsweb.com/~dav4is/people/GRIS193.htm
http://memory.loc.gov/ammem/today/may24.html
http://www.msnbc.msn.com/id/11147506/
http://en.wikipedia.org/wiki/Dallas%2C_Texas#History
http://p2.www.britannica.com/ebc/article-9320912

Chapter 12: Millard Fillmore
Tally, Steve, *Bland Ambition*, Orlando, Harcourt Brace Jovanovich, 1992, pp 95-100
Barzman, Sol, *Madmen and Geniuses*, Chicago, Follett, 1974, pp 84-89
Witcover, Jules, *Crapshoot: Rolling the Dice on the Vice Presidency*, New York, Crown, 1992
Vice Presidents: A Biographical Dictionary, New York, Checkmark Books, 2001, L. Edward Purcell, editor,
    by Dieter C. Ullruch, pp 113-121
Harwood, Michael, *In the Shadow of Presidents*, New York, J.B. Lippincott, 1966, pp 68-74
Young, Donald, *American Roulette: The History and Dilemma of the Vice Presidency*,
    New York, Holt, Rinehart and Winston, 1965, pp 55-65
http://www.whitehouse.gov/history/presidents/mf13.html
http://www.senate.gov/reference/common/generic/Profiles_THB.htm
http://en.wikipedia.org/wiki/Thomas_Hart_Benton_%28senator%29
http://www.americanpresidents.org/presidents/president.asp?PresidentNumber=13
http://en.wikipedia.org/wiki/Millard_Fillmore
http://en.wikipedia.org/wiki/Compromise_of_1850

http://www.senate.gov/artandhistory/history/minute/Bitter_Feelings_In_the_Senate_
    Chamber.htm
http://www.jfklibrary.org/Education+and+Public+Programs/Profile+in+Courage+Award/
    Profiles+in+Courage.htm
http://en.wikipedia.org/wiki/Compromise_of_1850
http://www.eleggua.com/History/1975.html

Chapter 13: William Rufus DeVane King
Tally, Steve, *Bland Ambition*, Orlando, Harcourt Brace Jovanovich, 1992, pp 101-106
Barzman, Sol, *Madmen and Geniuses*, Chicago, Follett, 1974, pp 90-95
Witcover, Jules, *Crapshoot: Rolling the Dice on the Vice Presidency*, New York, Crown, 1992
http://www.millercenter.virginia.edu/Ampres/essays/pierce/biography/2
http://www.senate.gov/artandhistory/history/resources/pdf/william_king.pdf
http://www.tompaine.com/Archive/scontent/2458.html
Loewen, James W., *Lies Across America*, New York, Touchstone, 2000, pp 367-370
http://www.alabamamoments.state.al.us/sec09.html
http://www.answers.com/topic/william-r-king
http://lindholm.jp/chinf_buc.html
http://en.wikipedia.org/wiki/Gay#Development_of_modern_usage

Chapter 14: John Cabell Breckinridge
Tally, Steve, *Bland Ambition*, Orlando, Harcourt Brace Jovanovich, 1992, pp 107-114
Barzman, Sol, *Madmen and Geniuses*, Chicago, Follett, 1974, pp 97-101
Witcover, Jules, *Crapshoot: Rolling the Dice on the Vice Presidency*, New York, Crown, 1992
Vice Presidents: A Biographical Dictionary, New York, Checkmark Books, 2001, L. Edward Purcell, editor,
    by John Marshall Hewitt, pp 129-137
http://www.doctorzebra.com/prez/a_breck.htm (from the New York Times, 12/7/1863)
http://en.wikipedia.org/wiki/John_C._Breckinridge
http://www.senate.gov/artandhistory/history/common/generic/VP_John_Breckinridge.htm
http://www.gutenberg.org/files/15394/15394-h/15394-h.htm
http://deadpresidentsdaily.blogspot.com/

Chapter 15: Hannibal Hamlin
Tally, Steve, *Bland Ambition*, Orlando, Harcourt Brace Jovanovich, 1992, pp 115-124
Barzman, Sol, *Madmen and Geniuses*, Chicago, Follett, 1974, pp 102-107
Witcover, Jules, *Crapshoot: Rolling the Dice on the Vice Presidency*, New York, Crown, 1992
Vice Presidents: A Biographical Dictionary, New York, Checkmark Books, 2001, L. Edward Purcell, editor,
    by H. Draper Hunt, pp 138-146
http://www.senate.gov/artandhistory/history/common/generic/VP_Hannibal_Hamlin.htm
http://en.wikipedia.org/wiki/Hannibal_Hamlin
http://www.nps.gov/anti/historyculture/photography.htm
http://en.wikipedia.org/wiki/Seaman_Recruit
http://www.usatrivia.com/pasnatt.html
http://www.nndb.com/people/184/000093902/
http://www.presidentsusa.net/campaignslogans.html

Chapter 16: Andrew Johnson
Tally, Steve, *Bland Ambition*, Orlando, Harcourt Brace Jovanovich, 1992, pp 130-140
Barzman, Sol, *Madmen and Geniuses*, Chicago, Follett, 1974, pp 108-113

Witcover, Jules, *Crapshoot: Rolling the Dice on the Vice Presidency*, New York, Crown, 1992
Vice Presidents: A Biographical Dictionary, New York, Checkmark Books, 2001,L. Edward Purcell, editor,
    by Richard Zuczec, pp 147-153
http://en.wikipedia.org/wiki/Fourteenth_Amendment_to_the_United_States_Constitution
http://encarta.msn.com/encyclopedia_761563281_4/Andrew_Johnson.html
http://en.wikipedia.org/wiki/Andrew_Johnson#Impeachment:_the_first_attempt
http://www.whitehouse.gov/history/presidents/aj17.html
http://en.wikipedia.org/wiki/George_Atzerodt
http://en.wikipedia.org/wiki/Abraham_Lincoln_assassination#Andrew_Johnson
http://www.law.umkc.edu/faculty/projects/ftrials/lincolnconspiracy/atzerodt.html
http://inaugural.senate.gov/history/daysevents/vpswearingin.htm
http://www.doctorzebra.com/prez/z_x17inaugural_g.htm
http://showcase.netins.net/web/creative/lincoln/speeches/inaug2.htm
http://en.wikipedia.org/wiki/John_Wilkes_Booth#Hatching_the_plot
http://en.wikipedia.org/wiki/Lewis_Payne
http://home.att.net/~rjnorton/Lincoln82.html
http://members.aol.com/RVSNorton/Lincoln27.html

Chapter 17: Schuyler Colfax

Tally, Steve, *Bland Ambition*, Orlando, Harcourt Brace Jovanovich, 1992, pp 141-145
Barzman, Sol, *Madmen and Geniuses*, Chicago, Follett, 1974, pp 114-120
Vice Presidents: A Biographical Dictionary, New York, Checkmark Books, 2001,L. Edward Purcell, editor,
    by Patrick J. Furlong and Anne Leonard, pp 154-161
Harwood, Michael, *In the Shadow of Presidents*, New York, J.B. Lippincott, 1966, pp 97-101
Young, Donald, *American Roulette: The History and Dilemma of the Vice Presidency*,
    New York, Holt, Rinehart and Winston, 1965, pp 83-88
http://www.senate.gov/artandhistory/history/common/generic/VP_Schuyler_Colfax.htm
http://en.wikipedia.org/wiki/Crédit_Mobilier
http://en.wikipedia.org/wiki/Oakes_Ames
http://en.wikipedia.org/wiki/Cr%C3%A9dit_Mobilier_of_America_scandal
http://www.infoplease.com/ce6/history/A0813974.html
http://www.pbs.org/wgbh/amex/tcrr/sfeature/sf_scandals.html
http://cprr.org/Museum/Crédit_Mobilier_1873.html
http://www.bartleby.com/65/cr/CréditMo.html
http://content.lib.washington.edu/curriculumpackets/homesteaders/Catalog1870.html
http://ap.grolier.com/article?assetid=0112820-00&templatename=/article/article.html
http://www.pbs.org/wgbh/amex/tcrr/peopleevents/e_scandal.html
http://www.cprr.org/Museum/Crédit_Mobilier.html
http://www.linecamp.com/museums/americanwest/western_clubs/union_pacific_railroad/
    union_pacific_railroad.html
http://www.harpweek.com/09Cartoon/BrowseByDateCartoon.asp?Month=March&Date=15
http://www.let.rug.nl/usa/E/ironhorse/ironhorse13.htm
http://en.wikipedia.org/wiki/First_Transcontinental_Railroad
http://en.wikipedia.org/wiki/Thomas_C._Durant
http://www.answers.com/topic/cr-dit-mobilier-of-america-scandal
http://www.senate.gov/artandhistory/history/resources/pdf/schulyer_colfax.pdf
http://en.wikipedia.org/wiki/Oakes_Ames

Chapter 18: Henry Wilson
Tally, Steve, *Bland Ambition*, Orlando, Harcourt Brace Jovanovich, 1992, pp 146-151
Barzman, Sol, *Madmen and Geniuses*, Chicago, Follett, 1974, pp 122-127
Witcover, Jules, *Crapshoot: Rolling the Dice on the Vice Presidency*, New York, Crown, 1992
Vice Presidents: A Biographical Dictionary, New York, Checkmark Books, 2001,L. Edward Purcell, editor,
    by Richard H. Abbott, pp 162-169
Harwood, Michael, *In the Shadow of Presidents*, New York, J.B. Lippincott, 1966, pp 102-108
Young, Donald, *American Roulette: The History and Dilemma of the Vice Presidency*,
    New York, Holt, Rinehart and Winston, 1965, pp 87-88
http://en.wikipedia.org/wiki/Henry_Wilson
http://bioguide.congress.gov/scripts/biodisplay.pl?index=W000585
http://www.senate.gov/artandhistory/history/resources/pdf/henry_wilson.pdf
http://www.uua.org/uuhs/duub/articles/horatioalgerjr.html
http://en.wikipedia.org/wiki/Henry_Wilson
http://www.highbeam.com/doc/1G1-6577716.html
http://www.colorado.edu/ibs/pubs/eb/eb2005-0009.pdf

Chapter 19: William Almon Wheeler
Tally, Steve, *Bland Ambition*, Orlando, Harcourt Brace Jovanovich, 1992, pp 152-156
Barzman, Sol, *Madmen and Geniuses*, Chicago, Follett, 1974, pp 128-132
Witcover, Jules, *Crapshoot: Rolling the Dice on the Vice Presidency*, New York, Crown, 1992
Vice Presidents: A Biographical Dictionary, New York, Checkmark Books, 2001,L. Edward Purcell, editor,
    by Frank P. Vazzano, pp 170-179
Harwood, Michael, *In the Shadow of Presidents*, New York, J.B. Lippincott, 1966, pp 109-112
Young, Donald, *American Roulette: The History and Dilemma of the Vice Presidency*,
    New York, Holt, Rinehart and Winston, 1965, pp 88-89
http://en.wikipedia.org/wiki/William_A._Wheeler
http://www.senate.gov/artandhistory/history/resources/pdf/william_wheeler.pdf
http://www.senate.gov/artandhistory/art/artifact/Sculpture_22_00019.htm#bio
http://famousamericans.net/williamhenrysmith/
http://en.wikipedia.org/wiki/United_States_presidential_election,_1876
http://www.senate.gov/artandhistory/history/common/generic/VP_William_Wheeler.htm

Chapter 20: Chester Arthur
Tally, Steve, *Bland Ambition*, Orlando, Harcourt Brace Jovanovich, 1992, pp 158-166
Barzman, Sol, *Madmen and Geniuses*, Chicago, Follett, 1974, pp 134-139
Witcover, Jules, *Crapshoot: Rolling the Dice on the Vice Presidency*, New York, Crown, 1992
Vice Presidents: A Biographical Dictionary, New York, Checkmark Books, 2001,L. Edward Purcell, editor,
    by James Doenecke, pp 178-185
Harwood, Michael, *In the Shadow of Presidents*, New York, J.B. Lippincott, 1966, pp 113-122
Young, Donald, *American Roulette: The History and Dilemma of the Vice Presidency*,
    New York, Holt, Rinehart and Winston, 1965, pp 89-110
http://www.whitehouse.gov/history/presidents/ca21.html
http://en.wikipedia.org/wiki/Chester_A._Arthur
http://www.senate.gov/artandhistory/history/resources/pdf/chester_arthur.pdf
http://home.nycap.rr.com/useless/garfield/index.html
http://www.historybuff.com/library/refgarfield.html
http://en.wikipedia.org/wiki/Charles_J._Guiteau
http://www.geocities.com/proprioter/y_guiteau.html

Chapter 21: Thomas Andrews Hendricks
Tally, Steve, *Bland Ambition*, Orlando, Harcourt Brace Jovanovich, 1992, pp 167-173
Barzman, Sol, *Madmen and Geniuses*, Chicago, Follett, 1974, pp 140-144
Witcover, Jules, *Crapshoot: Rolling the Dice on the Vice Presidency*, New York, Crown, 1992
Vice Presidents: A Biographical Dictionary, New York, Checkmark Books, 2001, L. Edward Purcell, editor;
    by Thomas Burnell Colbert, pp 186-193
Harwood, Michael, *In the Shadow of Presidents*, New York, J.B. Lippincott, 1966, pp 123-129
http://bioguide.congress.gov/scripts/biodisplay.pl?index=H000493
http://en.wikipedia.org/wiki/Thomas_A._Hendricks
http://www.u-s-history.com/pages/h745.html
http://en.wikipedia.org/wiki/Presidential_Succession_Act#Presidential_Succession_Act_
    of_1792
http://www.senate.gov/artandhistory/history/minute/Presidential_Succession_Act.htm
http://en.wikipedia.org/wiki/United_States_presidential_election,_1880
http://en.wikipedia.org/wiki/Samuel_Tilden
http://www.whitehousehistory.org/02/subs/02_b.html
http://www.senate.gov/artandhistory/history/common/generic/VP_Thomas_Hendricks.htm

Chapter 22: Levi Parsons Morton
Tally, Steve, *Bland Ambition*, Orlando, Harcourt Brace Jovanovich, 1992, pp 174-178
Barzman, Sol, *Madmen and Geniuses*, Chicago, Follett, 1974, pp 146-151
Witcover, Jules, *Crapshoot: Rolling the Dice on the Vice Presidency*, New York, Crown, 1992
Vice Presidents: A Biographical Dictionary, New York, Checkmark Books, 2001, L. Edward Purcell, editor;
    by Robert S. LaForte, pp 194-203
Harwood, Michael, *In the Shadow of Presidents*, New York, J.B. Lippincott, 1966, pp 130-133
http://bioguide.congress.gov/scripts/biodisplay.pl?index=M001018
http://www.senate.gov/artandhistory/history/common/generic/VP_Levi_Morton.htm
http://en.wikipedia.org/wiki/Levi_P._Morton

Chapter 23: Adlai Ewing Stevenson
Tally, Steve, *Bland Ambition*, Orlando, Harcourt Brace Jovanovich, 1992, pp 184-189
Barzman, Sol, *Madmen and Geniuses*, Chicago, Follett, 1974, pp 152-157
Witcover, Jules, *Crapshoot: Rolling the Dice on the Vice Presidency*, New York, Crown, 1992
Vice Presidents: A Biographical Dictionary, New York, Checkmark Books, 2001, L. Edward Purcell, editor;
    by Leonard C. Schlup, pp 204-215
Harwood, Michael, *In the Shadow of Presidents*, New York, J.B. Lippincott, 1966, pp 134-137
http://en.wikipedia.org/wiki/Adlai_E._Stevenson
http://www.senate.gov/artandhistory/history/resources/pdf/adlai_stevenson.pdf
http://72.14.253.104/search?q=cache:kS6P4HUsoDYJ:www.cr.nps.gov/history/online_books/
    albright2/pdf/ch8.pdf+adlai+stevenson+naming+mt+rainier&hl=en&ct=clnk&cd=1
    &gl=us
http://www.time.com/time/magazine/article/0,9171,719616-3,00.html
http://www.time.com/time/magazine/article/0,9171,719616-2,00.html
http://en.wikipedia.org/wiki/Tacoma#History
http://www.senate.gov/artandhistory/history/common/generic/VP_Adlai_Stevenson.htm
http://en.wikipedia.org/wiki/United_States_presidential_election,_1856
http://en.wikipedia.org/wiki/United_States_presidential_election,_1860
http://en.wikipedia.org/wiki/United_States_presidential_election,_1864
http://en.wikipedia.org/wiki/United_States_presidential_election,_1868

http://en.wikipedia.org/wiki/United_States_presidential_election,_1872
http://en.wikipedia.org/wiki/United_States_presidential_election,_1876
http://en.wikipedia.org/wiki/United_States_presidential_election,_1880
http://en.wikipedia.org/wiki/United_States_presidential_election,_1884
http://en.wikipedia.org/wiki/United_States_presidential_election,_1888
http://encarta.msn.com/encyclopedia_761554156_3/Grover_Cleveland.html
http://en.wikipedia.org/wiki/United_States_presidential_election,_1892
http://en.wikipedia.org/wiki/Adlai_Stevenson#1952_presidential_bid
http://en.wikipedia.org/wiki/Panic_of_1893

Chapter 24: Garret Augustus Hobart
Tally, Steve, *Bland Ambition*, Orlando, Harcourt Brace Jovanovich, 1992, pp 190-195
Barzman, Sol, *Madmen and Geniuses*, Chicago, Follett, 1974, pp 158-163
Witcover, Jules, *Crapshoot: Rolling the Dice on the Vice Presidency*, New York, Crown, 1992
Vice Presidents: A Biographical Dictionary, New York, Checkmark Books, 2001, L. Edward Purcell, editor,
    by Leonard C. Schlup, pp 216-225
Harwood, Michael, *In the Shadow of Presidents*, New York, J.B. Lippincott, 1966, pp 138-143
Chandler Waldrup, Carole, *The Vice Presidents*, Jefferson, NC, McFarland, 2006, pp 141-144
http://en.wikipedia.org/wiki/Garret_Hobart
http://www.senate.gov/artandhistory/history/common/generic/VP_Garret_Hobart.htm
http://en.wikipedia.org/wiki/Spanish-American_War
http://en.wikipedia.org/wiki/William_Mckinley

Chapter 25: Theodore Roosevelt
Tally, Steve, *Bland Ambition*, Orlando, Harcourt Brace Jovanovich, 1992, pp 269-277
Barzman, Sol, *Madmen and Geniuses*, Chicago, Follett, 1974, pp 229-235
Witcover, Jules, *Crapshoot: Rolling the Dice on the Vice Presidency*, New York, Crown, 1992
Vice Presidents: A Biographical Dictionary, New York, Checkmark Books, 2001, L. Edward Purcell, editor,
    by Mark L. Kleinman, pp 297-305
Harwood, Michael, *In the Shadow of Presidents*, New York, J.B. Lippincott, 1966, pp 181-185
Young, Donald, *American Roulette: The History and Dilemma of the Vice Presidency*,
    New York, Holt, Rinehart and Winston, 1965, pp 174-195
Chandler Waldrup, Carole, *The Vice Presidents*, Jefferson, NC, McFarland, 2006, pp 189-194
http://www.theodoreroosevelt.org/
http://en.wikipedia.org/wiki/Theodore_Roosevelt
http://en.wikipedia.org/wiki/Theodore_roosevelt#Media
http://www.squidoo.com/theodorerooseveltjr/
http://www.senate.gov/artandhistory/history/common/generic/VP_Theodore_Roosevelt.
    htm
http://www.deadwood.searchroots.com/bullock.htm
    April 16, 1897: T. Roosevelt Appointed Assistant Secretary of the Navy. Crucible of
    Empire - Timeline. PBS Online. Retrieved on 2007-07-26.
    Transcript For "Crucible Of Empire." Crucible of Empire - Timeline. PBS Online.
    Retrieved on 2007-07-26.
http://en.wikipedia.org/wiki/Alice_Roosevelt_Longworth
http://www.salon.com/people/feature/1999/06/07/longworth/
http://nmnm.essortment.com/aliceroosevelt_rxlk.htm

http://www.rgj.com/news/stories/html/2004/03/06/65599.php
http://www.gvsu.edu/hauenstein/index.cfm?id=A3543CF2-F961-4CD4-
    4C4AFBC87182D08D

Chapter 26: Charles Fairlbanks
Tally, Steve, *Bland Ambition*, Orlando, Harcourt Brace Jovanovich, 1992, pp 208-213
Barzman, Sol, *Madmen and Geniuses*, Chicago, Follett, 1974, pp 174-180
Witcover, Jules, *Crapshoot: Rolling the Dice on the Vice Presidency*, New York, Crown, 1992
Vice Presidents: A Biographical Dictionary, New York, Checkmark Books, 2001, L. Edward Purcell, editor;
    by Ray E. Boomhower, pp 237-241
Harwood, Michael, *In the Shadow of Presidents*, New York, J.B. Lippincott, 1966, pp 149-155
Chandler Waldrup, Carole, *The Vice Presidents*, Jefferson, NC, McFarland, 2006, pp 152-155
http://www.senate.gov/artandhistory/history/common/generic/VP_Charles_Fairbanks.htm
http://en.wikipedia.org/wiki/Charles_W._Fairbanks
http://en.wikipedia.org/wiki/United_States_presidential_election,_1916

Chapter 27: James Schoolcraft Sherman
Tally, Steve, *Bland Ambition*, Orlando, Harcourt Brace Jovanovich, 1992, pp 214-219
Barzman, Sol, *Madmen and Geniuses*, Chicago, Follett, 1974, pp 182-187
Witcover, Jules, *Crapshoot: Rolling the Dice on the Vice Presidency*, New York, Crown, 1992
Vice Presidents: A Biographical Dictionary, New York, Checkmark Books, 2001, L. Edward Purcell, editor;
    by William H. Cumberland, pp 242-250
Harwood, Michael, *In the Shadow of Presidents*, New York, J.B. Lippincott, 1966, pp 152-155
Chandler Waldrup, Carole, *The Vice Presidents*, Jefferson, NC, McFarland, 2006, pp 156-159
http://en.wikipedia.org/wiki/James_S._Sherman
http://www.answers.com/topic/ragtime-7
http://www.senate.gov/artandhistory/history/common/generic/VP_James_Sherman.htm
http://en.wikipedia.org/wiki/United_States_presidential_election,_1912
http://www.guardian.co.uk/US_election_race/Story/0,,344613,00.html/

Chapter 28: Thomas Riley Marshall
Tally, Steve, *Bland Ambition*, Orlando, Harcourt Brace Jovanovich, 1992, pp 220-229
Barzman, Sol, *Madmen and Geniuses*, Chicago, Follett, 1974, pp 188-195
Witcover, Jules, *Crapshoot: Rolling the Dice on the Vice Presidency*, New York, Crown, 1992
Vice Presidents: A Biographical Dictionary, New York, Checkmark Books, 2001, L. Edward Purcell, editor;
    by Peter T. Harstad, pp 251-261
Harwood, Michael, *In the Shadow of Presidents*, New York, J.B. Lippincott, 1966, pp 156-163
Young, Donald, *American Roulette: The History and Dilemma of the Vice Presidency*,
    New York, Holt, Rinehart and Winston, 1965, pp 125-144
Chandler Waldrup, Carole, *The Vice Presidents*, Jefferson, NC, McFarland, 2006, pp 160-165
http://en.wikipedia.org/wiki/Thomas_R._Marshall
http://en.wikipedia.org/wiki/Oscar_W._Underwood
http://www.senate.gov/artandhistory/history/common/generic/VP_Thomas_Marshall.htm
http://en.wikipedia.org/wiki/Treaty_of_Versailles#Reaction_to_the_treaty

Chapter 29: Calvin Coolidge
Tally, Steve, *Bland Ambition*, Orlando, Harcourt Brace Jovanovich, 1992, pp 230-238
Barzman, Sol, *Madmen and Geniuses*, Chicago, Follett, 1974, pp 196-202
Witcover, Jules, *Crapshoot: Rolling the Dice on the Vice Presidency*, New York, Crown, 1992

Vice Presidents: A Biographical Dictionary, New York, Checkmark Books, 2001,L. Edward Purcell, editor;
   by Paul L. Silver, pp 262-271
Young, Donald, *American Roulette: The History and Dilemma of the Vice Presidency*,
   New York, Holt, Rinehart and Winston, 1965, pp 125-144
Harwood, Michael, *In the Shadow of Presidents*, New York, J.B. Lippincott, 1966, pp 164-168
Chandler Waldrup, Carole, *The Vice Presidents*, Jefferson, NC, McFarland, 2006, pp 166-171
http://en.wikipedia.org/wiki/Calvin_Coolidge#Vice_Presidency
http://en.wikipedia.org/wiki/Warren_G._Harding#Personal_scandals_and_allegations
http://en.wikipedia.org/wiki/Ohio_Gang
http://www.ohiohistorycentral.org/entry.php?rec=199
http://www.doctorzebra.com/prez/z_x29wilbur_g.htm
http://en.wikipedia.org/wiki/Albert_B._Fall
http://www.christianitytoday.com/books/features/bookwk/040209.html
http://en.wikipedia.org/wiki/1920_Republican_National_Convention#Tenth_ballot
http://www2.ljworld.com/news/2003/nov/24/text_of_richard2/

Chapter 30: Charles Gates Dawes

Tally, Steve, *Bland Ambition*, Orlando, Harcourt Brace Jovanovich, 1992, pp 239-248
Barzman, Sol, *Madmen and Geniuses*, Chicago, Follett, 1974, pp 204-210
Witcover, Jules, *Crapshoot: Rolling the Dice on the Vice Presidency*, New York, Crown, 1992
Vice Presidents: A Biographical Dictionary, New York, Checkmark Books, 2001,L. Edward Purcell, editor;
   by Robert A. Waller, pp 272-281
Harwood, Michael, *In the Shadow of Presidents*, New York, J.B. Lippincott, 1966, pp 169-172
Young, Donald, *American Roulette: The History and Dilemma of the Vice Presidency*,
   New York, Holt, Rinehart and Winston, 1965, pp 154-161
Chandler Waldrup, Carole, *The Vice Presidents*, Jefferson, NC, McFarland, 2006, pp 172-177
http://en.wikipedia.org/wiki/Charles_G._Dawes
http://www.senate.gov/artandhistory/history/common/generic/VP_Charles_Dawes.htm
http://en.wikipedia.org/wiki/Dawes_Plan
http://en.wikipedia.org/wiki/William_Edgar_Borah
http://en.wikipedia.org/wiki/Treaty_of_Versailles

Chapter 31: Charles Curtis

Tally, Steve, *Bland Ambition*, Orlando, Harcourt Brace Jovanovich, 1992, pp 249-255
Barzman, Sol, *Madmen and Geniuses*, Chicago, Follett, 1974, pp 212-218
Witcover, Jules, *Crapshoot: Rolling the Dice on the Vice Presidency*, New York, Crown, 1992
Vice Presidents: A Biographical Dictionary, New York, Checkmark Books, 2001,L. Edward Purcell, editor;
   by Willam E. Unrau, pp 283-288
Harwood, Michael, *In the Shadow of Presidents*, New York, J.B. Lippincott, 1966, pp 173-175
Young, Donald, *American Roulette: The History and Dilemma of the Vice Presidency*,
   New York, Holt, Rinehart and Winston, 1965, pp 161-162
Chandler Waldrup, Carole, *The Vice Presidents*, Jefferson, NC, McFarland, 2006, pp 178-182
http://www.senate.gov/artandhistory/history/common/generic/VP_Charles_Curtis.htm
http://en.wikipedia.org/wiki/Charles_Curtis
http://www.whitehouse.gov/history/presidents/cc30.html
http://en.wikipedia.org/wiki/United_States_presidential_election,_1928
http://www.time.com/time/magazine/article/0,9171,889620-1,00.html
http://www.time.com/time/magazine/article/0,9171,737392,00.html
http://en.wikipedia.org/wiki/United_States_presidential_election,_1932

Chapter 32: John Nance Garner
Tally, Steve, *Bland Ambition*, Orlando, Harcourt Brace Jovanovich, 1992, pp 261-268
Barzman, Sol, *Madmen and Geniuses*, Chicago, Follett, 1974, pp 220-227
Witcover, Jules, *Crapshoot: Rolling the Dice on the Vice Presidency*, New York, Crown, 1992
Vice Presidents: A Biographical Dictionary, New York, Checkmark Books, 2001, L. Edward Purcell, editor;
    by J. Kent Calder, pp 289-295
Harwood, Michael, *In the Shadow of Presidents*, New York, J.B. Lippincott, 1966, pp 176-180
Young, Donald, *American Roulette: The History and Dilemma of the Vice Presidency*,
    New York, Holt, Rinehart and Winston, 1965, pp 163-173
Chandler Waldrup, Carole, *The Vice Presidents*, Jefferson, NC, McFarland, 2006, pp 183-188
http://en.wikipedia.org/wiki/John_Nance_Garner
http://www.time.com/time/magazine/article/0,9171,895752,00.html?promoid=googlep
http://en.wikipedia.org/wiki/Alf_Landon
http://www.senate.gov/artandhistory/history/common/generic/VP_John_Garner.htm
http://en.wikipedia.org/wiki/Slogan
http://www.time.com/time/magazine/article/0,9171,756709,00.html
http://en.wikipedia.org/wiki/Roy_A._Roberts
http://en.wikipedia.org/wiki/Superman:_War_of_the_Worlds
http://en.wikipedia.org/wiki/Giuseppe_Zangara
http://www.nytimes.com/2006/07/02/weekinreview/02goodheart.html?pagewanted=2&ei=5
    070&en=1e19fda26522a567&ex=1172552400
http://en.wikiquote.org/wiki/John_Nance_Garner
http://www.time.com/time/magazine/article/0,9171,761057,00.html
http://en.wikipedia.org/wiki/Marian_Anderson

Chapter 33: Henry Agard Wallace
Tally, Steve, *Bland Ambition*, Orlando, Harcourt Brace Jovanovich, 1992, pp 269-277
Barzman, Sol, *Madmen and Geniuses*, Chicago, Follett, 1974, pp 229-235
Witcover, Jules, *Crapshoot: Rolling the Dice on the Vice Presidency*, New York, Crown, 1992
Vice Presidents: A Biographical Dictionary, New York, Checkmark Books, 2001, L. Edward Purcell, editor;
    by Mark L. Kleinman, pp 297-305
Harwood, Michael, *In the Shadow of Presidents*, New York, J.B. Lippincott, 1966, pp 181-185
Young, Donald, *American Roulette: The History and Dilemma of the Vice Presidency*,
    New York, Holt, Rinehart and Winston, 1965, pp 174-195
Chandler Waldrup, Carole, *The Vice Presidents*, Jefferson, NC, McFarland, 2006, pp 189-194
http://hometown.aol.com/thejman99/book.html
http://www.cooperativeindividualism.org/schlesinger_wallace_bio.html
http://www.conspiracyarchive.com/NWO/All_Seeing_Eye.htm
http://en.wikipedia.org/wiki/Henry_A._Wallace
http://www.juntosociety.com/vp/hwallace.html
http://www.senate.gov/artandhistory/history/common/generic/VP_Henry_Wallace.htm
http://libertyunbound.com/archive/2002_06/cox-druids.html
http://en.wikipedia.org/wiki/Great_White_Brotherhood
http://www.culturevulture.net/books/AmericanDreamer.htm
http://www.findarticles.com/p/articles/mi_m1282/is_n14_v46/ai_15674708
http://www.trivia-library.com/c/history-of-the-search-for-shambhala-part-4.htm
http://www.time.com/time/magazine/article/0,9171,888412,00.html?promoid=googlep
http://www.h-net.org/reviews/showrev.cgi?path=532956170440

http://www.time.com/time/magazine/article/0,9171,764253,00.html

Chapter 34: Harry S Truman
Tally, Steve, *Bland Ambition*, Orlando, Harcourt Brace Jovanovich, 1992, pp 278-287
Barzman, Sol, *Madmen and Geniuses*, Chicago, Follett, 1974, pp 236-243
Witcover, Jules, *Crapshoot: Rolling the Dice on the Vice Presidency*, New York, Crown, 1992
Vice Presidents: A Biographical Dictionary, New York, Checkmark Books, 2001, L. Edward Purcell, editor,
    by Robert H. Farrell, pp 306-313
Harwood, Michael, *In the Shadow of Presidents*, New York, J.B. Lippincott, 1966, pp 186-195
Young, Donald, *American Roulette: The History and Dilemma of the Vice Presidency*,
    New York, Holt, Rinehart and Winston, 1965, pp 196-251
Chandler Waldrup, Carole, *The Vice Presidents*, Jefferson, NC, McFarland, 2006, pp 195-201
Boller Jr., Paul F., *Presidential Anecdotes*, New York, Penguin, 1981, pp 278-289
Beschloss, Michael, *Newsweek*, 5/14/2007, "A Case Of Courage," pp 32-37
http://www.time.com/time/magazine/article/0,9171,764253,00.html
http://www.senate.gov/artandhistory/history/common/generic/VP_Harry_Truman.htm
http://en.wikipedia.org/wiki/Historical_rankings_of_United_States_Presidents
http://www.commondreams.org/views06/0302-24.htm
http://oregonstate.edu/cla/polisci/faculty/sahr/sahr.htm
http://www.time.com/time/magazine/article/0,9171,819395,00.html
http://www.washingtonpost.com/ac2/wp-dyn?pagename=article&node=&contentId=
    A19305-2001Nov26
http://en.wikipedia.org/wiki/Harry_S._Truman
http://www.infoplease.com/askeds/truman-middle-name.html
http://www.trumanlibrary.org/speriod.htm
http://www.time.com/time/magazine/article/0,9171,815031,00.html

Chapter 35: Alben W. Barkley
Tally, Steve, *Bland Ambition*, Orlando, Harcourt Brace Jovanovich, 1992, pp 269-277
Barzman, Sol, *Madmen and Geniuses*, Chicago, Follett, 1974, pp 229-235
Witcover, Jules, *Crapshoot: Rolling the Dice on the Vice Presidency*, New York, Crown, 1992
Vice Presidents: A Biographical Dictionary, New York, Checkmark Books, 2001, L. Edward Purcell, editor,
    by Mark L. Kleinman, pp 297-305
Harwood, Michael, *In the Shadow of Presidents*, New York, J.B. Lippincott, 1966, pp 181-185
Young, Donald, *American Roulette: The History and Dilemma of the Vice Presidency*,
    New York, Holt, Rinehart and Winston, 1965, pp 174-195
Chandler Waldrup, Carole, *The Vice Presidents*, Jefferson, NC, McFarland, 2006, pp 189-194
http://www.historybuff.com/library/reftruman.html
http://en.wikipedia.org/wiki/Alben_W._Barkley
http://www.senate.gov/artandhistory/history/common/generic/VP_Alben_Barkley.htm
http://www.time.com/time/magazine/article/0,9171,817157,00.html?promoid=googlep
http://www.time.com/time/magazine/article/0,9171,817954,00.html?promoid=googlep
http://en.wikipedia.org/wiki/Give_'em_Hell,_Harry!
http://www.trumanlibrary.org/oralhist/davidsn2.htm

Chapter 36: Richard M. Nixon
Tally, Steve, *Bland Ambition*, Orlando, Harcourt Brace Jovanovich, 1992, pp 295-312
Barzman, Sol, *Madmen and Geniuses*, Chicago, Follett, 1974, pp 252-260
Witcover, Jules, *Crapshoot: Rolling the Dice on the Vice Presidency*, New York, Crown, 1992

Vice Presidents: A Biographical Dictionary, New York, Checkmark Books, 2001, L. Edward Purcell, editor,
   by Joan Hoff, pp 322-331
Harwood, Michael, *In the Shadow of Presidents*, New York, J.B. Lippincott, 1966, pp 200-206
Young, Donald, *American Roulette: The History and Dilemma of the Vice Presidency*,
   New York, Holt, Rinehart and Winston, 1965, pp 252-285
Chandler Waldrup, Carole, *The Vice Presidents*, Jefferson, NC, McFarland, 2006, pp 207-213
http://www.senate.gov/artandhistory/history/common/generic/VP_Richard_Nixon.htm
http://en.wikipedia.org/wiki/U.S._presidential_election,_1960
http://en.wikiquote.org/wiki/Richard_Nixon
http://www.cjasmonthly.com/august_nixon.html
http://en.wikipedia.org/wiki/Dwight_eisenhower

Chapter 37: Lyndon Baines Johnson
Tally, Steve, *Bland Ambition*, Orlando, Harcourt Brace Jovanovich, 1992, pp 313-322
Barzman, Sol, *Madmen and Geniuses*, Chicago, Follett, 1974, pp 252-260
Witcover, Jules, *Crapshoot: Rolling the Dice on the Vice Presidency*, New York, Crown, 1992
Vice Presidents: A Biographical Dictionary, New York, Checkmark Books, 2001, L. Edward Purcell, editor,
   by G.L. Seligman, pp 332-340
Harwood, Michael, *In the Shadow of Presidents*, New York, J.B. Lippincott, 1966, pp 207-213
Young, Donald, *American Roulette: The History and Dilemma of the Vice Presidency*,
   New York, Holt, Rinehart and Winston, 1965, pp 286-311
Chandler Waldrup, Carole, *The Vice Presidents*, Jefferson, NC, McFarland, 2006, pp 207-213
http://en.wikipedia.org/wiki/Lyndon_Baines_Johnson#Vice_Presidency
http://www.pbs.org/wgbh/amex/presidents/36_1_johnson/filmmore/filmscript.html
http://indomitus.net/ir20040926.htm
http://www.ncc-1776.org/tle2005/tle339-20051002-05.html
http://www.badattitudes.com/Organ.pdf
http://tafkac.org/politics/lbj_penis.html
http://www.findarticles.com/p/articles/mi_m1316/is_n10_v29/ai_19898073
http://www.eiu.edu/~historia/1999/texas99.htm
http://archives.cjr.org/year/02/3/sherman.asp
http://www.time.com/time/magazine/article/0,9171,915245,00.html
http://www.harpers.org/NoAppeal.html
Beyer, Rick, *The Greatest Presidential Stories Never Told*, New York, Collins, 2007

Chapter 38: Hubert Humphrey
Tally, Steve, *Bland Ambition*, Orlando, Harcourt Brace Jovanovich, 1992, pp 323-334
Barzman, Sol, *Madmen and Geniuses*, Chicago, Follett, 1974, pp 272-280
Witcover, Jules, *Crapshoot: Rolling the Dice on the Vice Presidency*, New York, Crown, 1992
Vice Presidents: A Biographical Dictionary, New York, Checkmark Books, 2001, L. Edward Purcell, editor,
   by Karen M. Hult, pp 341-349
Harwood, Michael, *In the Shadow of Presidents*, New York, J.B. Lippincott, 1966, pp 214-217
Young, Donald, *American Roulette: The History and Dilemma of the Vice Presidency*,
   New York, Holt, Rinehart and Winston, 1965, pp 252-285
Chandler Waldrup, Carole, *The Vice Presidents*, Jefferson, NC, McFarland, 2006, pp 207-213
http://www.senate.gov/artandhistory/history/minute/Civil_Rights_Filibuster_Ended.htm
http://en.wikipedia.org/wiki/Hubert_Humphrey
http://en.wikipedia.org/wiki/Dixiecrat
http://www.senate.gov/artandhistory/history/common/generic/VP_Hubert_Humphrey.htm

http://www.time.com/time/magazine/article/0,9171,780085-6,00.html
http://www.msnbc.msn.com/id/7005168/
http://www.time.com/time/magazine/article/0,9171,998138-1,00.html
http://www.answers.com/topic/hubert-humphrey-1

Chapter 39: Spiro Agnew
Tally, Steve, *Bland Ambition*, Orlando, Harcourt Brace Jovanovich, 1992, pp 335-344
Barzman, Sol, *Madmen and Geniuses*, Chicago, Follett, 1974, pp 282-291
Witcover, Jules, *Crapshoot: Rolling the Dice on the Vice Presidency*, New York, Crown, 1992
Vice Presidents: A Biographical Dictionary, New York, Checkmark Books, 2001, L. Edward Purcell, editor,
    by John Robert Greene, pp 350-355
http://www.golfweb.com/u/ce/multi/0,1977,1919221,00.html
http://www.buzzle.com/editorials/4-16-2002-16690.ªsp
Witcover, Jules, *Crapshoot: Rolling the Dice on the Vice Presidency*, New York, Crown, 1992
Walth, Brent, *Fire at Eden's Gate*, Portland, Oregon Historical Society Press, 1995
http://en.wikipedia.org/wiki/Spiro_Agnew
http://www.goodbyemag.com/sep/agnew.htm
http://www.senate.gov/artandhistory/history/common/generic/VP_Spiro_Agnew.htm
http://www.answers.com/topic/spiro-agnew

Chapter 40: Gerald Ford
Tally, Steve, *Bland Ambition*, Orlando, Harcourt Brace Jovanovich, 1992, pp 345-353
Barzman, Sol, *Madmen and Geniuses*, Chicago, Follett, 1974, pp 292-300
Witcover, Jules, *Crapshoot: Rolling the Dice on the Vice Presidency*, New York, Crown, 1992
Vice Presidents: A Biographical Dictionary, New York, Checkmark Books, 2001, L. Edward Purcell, editor,
    by John Robert Greene, pp 356-361
http://www.theleftcoaster.com/archives/001911.php
http://www.thedesertsun.com/apps/pbcs.dll/article?AID=/20060422/
    SPORTS05/604220341/1071/COLUMNS05
http://www.classroomhelp.com/lessons/Presidents/ford.html
http://www.school-for-champions.com/history/geraldford.htm
http://www.npr.org/templates/story/story.php?storyId=1246185 (see book, "First Off The Tee"
    by Don Van Natta; claims in NPR story that "He hit many, many people with golf
    balls and took a lot of ribbing from Bob Hope and many other comedians, Chevy
    Chase among them.")
http://www.angelfire.com/de/classicalstories/page3.html
http://en.wikipedia.org/wiki/Gerald_Ford#House_of_Representatives
Beyer, Rick, *The Greatest Presidential Stories Never Told*, New York, Collins, 2007

Chapter 41: Nelson Aldrich Rockefeller
Tally, Steve, *Bland Ambition*, Orlando, Harcourt Brace Jovanovich, 1992, pp 345-353
Witcover, Jules, *Crapshoot: Rolling the Dice on the Vice Presidency*, New York, Crown, 1992
Vice Presidents: A Biographical Dictionary, New York, Checkmark Books, 2001, L. Edward Purcell, editor,
    editor; by Larry G. Dorsey, pp 362-372
http://www.ishipress.com/marshak.htm
http://en.wikipedia.org/wiki/Megan_Marshak
http://www.senate.gov/artandhistory/history/common/generic/VP_Gerald_Ford.htm
http://en.wikipedia.org/wiki/Nelson_Rockefeller
http://www.senate.gov/artandhistory/history/common/generic/VP_Nelson_Rockefeller.htm
http://en.wikipedia.org/wiki/Republican_National_Committee#Chairpersons_of_the_

Republican_National_Committee
http://www.nevadalabor.com/barbwire/barbo1/barb11-25-01.html
http://www.time.com/time/magazine/article/0,9171,922819-2,00.html
http://en.wikipedia.org/wiki/Sara_Jane_Moore
Imus in the Morning, Doris Kearns Goodwin guest, 1997 (?)
http://en.wikipedia.org/wiki/Sara_Jane_Moore

Chapter 42: Walter Mondale
Tally, Steve, *Bland Ambition*, Orlando, Harcourt Brace Jovanovich, 1992, pp 345-353
Witcover, Jules, *Crapshoot: Rolling the Dice on the Vice Presidency*, New York, Crown, 1992
Vice Presidents: A Biographical Dictionary, New York, Checkmark Books, 2001, L. Edward Purcell, editor,
    by Larry G. Dorsey, pp 362-372
http://en.wikipedia.org/wiki/Jimmy_Carter#Energy_crisis
http://www.senate.gov/artandhistory/history/common/generic/VP_Walter_Mondale.htm\

Chapter 43: George Herbert Walker Bush
Tally, Steve, *Bland Ambition*, Orlando, Harcourt Brace Jovanovich, 1992, pp 345-353
Witcover, Jules, *Crapshoot: Rolling the Dice on the Vice Presidency*, New York, Crown, 1992
Vice Presidents: A Biographical Dictionary, New York, Checkmark Books, 2001, L. Edward Purcell, editor,
    by Larry G. Dorsey, pp 383-392
http://www.senate.gov/artandhistory/history/common/generic/VP_George_Bush.htm
http://en.wikipedia.org/wiki/Iran-Contra_Affair
http://en.wikipedia.org/wiki/U.S._presidential_election,_1988#Republican_Party_
    nomination
http://www.time.com/time/magazine/article/0,9171,956828-6,00.html
http://www.nypost.com/seven/10042006/gossip/liz/gracious_politicians_amuse_liz_liz_
    smith.htm
http://www.pbs.org/newshour/character/essays/bush.html

Chapter 44: J. Danforth Quayle
Tally, Steve, *Bland Ambition*, Orlando, Harcourt Brace Jovanovich, 1992, pp 389-399
Witcover, Jules, *Crapshoot: Rolling the Dice on the Vice Presidency*, New York, Crown, 1992
Vice Presidents: A Biographical Dictionary, New York, Checkmark Books, 2001, L. Edward Purcell, editor,
    by Shirley Warshaw, pp 393-400
http://www.senate.gov/artandhistory/history/common/generic/VP_George_Bush.htm
http://www.quotationspage.com/quotes/Dan_Quayle/
http://www.snopes.com/quotes/quayle.htm
http://www.realchange.org/quayle.htm#quotes
http://www.bartleby.com/cgi-bin/texis/webinator/sitesearch?FILTER=&query=dan+quayle
    &x=0&y=0
http://www.realchange.org/quayle.htm
http://www.chara.gsu.edu/~gudehus/Quotations/quotations_opq.html (this one's
    questionable; he seems legitimate and cites many of his sources, but he has at least
    one quote that was debunked on snopes.com) NOTE: Donald Gudehus is a Physics
    & Astronomy Professor at Georgia State University with Eugene connections. Oh,
    and he quotes Queensryche on his page.
http://www.debates.org/pages/trans88c.html
http://homepages.cs.ncl.ac.uk/chris.holt/home.informal/bar/corsair.afdq/quayle.quotes/
    womens.issues.html Not fully corroborated. Have seen it reprinted several times, but

no one can cite the specific source. However, it's also not on the Snopes.com list of
"Quayleisms," or false Quayle quotes.
http://en.wikiquote.org/wiki/Dan_Quayle
http://www.ku.edu/~edit/danquotes.html
http://www.capitalcentury.com/1992.html
http://www.senate.gov/artandhistory/history/common/generic/VP_Dan_Quayle.htm
http://en.wikipedia.org/wiki/Senator,_you_are_no_Jack_Kennedy
http://www.npr.org/templates/story/story.php?storyId=4609218

Chapter 45: Albert Gore
Vice Presidents: A Biographical Dictionary, New York, Checkmark Books, 2001, L. Edward Purcell, editor,
    by Scott W. Rager, pp 401-412
http://www.senate.gov/artandhistory/history/common/generic/VP_Albert_Gore.htm
http://en.wikipedia.org/wiki/PMRC
http://archives.cnn.com/2000/ALLPOLITICS/stories/10/18/pres.debate/index.html
http://en.wikipedia.org/wiki/Terry_McAuliffe
Morning Edition, NPR "The Long View" segment, 4/26/07

Chapter 46: Richard Bruce "Dick" Cheney
http://www.thepittsburghchannel.com/news/2693558/detail.html
http://www.hsus.org/legislation_laws/wayne_pacelle_the_animal_advocate/cheneys_
    canned_kill_and_other_hunting_excesses_of_the_bush_administration.html
http://www.thesmokinggun.com/archive/021306icheney1.html
http://www.rollingstone.com/politics/story/6450422/the_curse_of_dick_cheney/
http://news.bbc.co.uk/2/hi/americas/4707354.stm
http://www.cnn.com/2006/POLITICS/02/14/cheney/index.html
Tally, Steve, *Bland Ambition*, Orlando, Harcourt Brace Jovanovich, 1992, pp 389-399
Witcover, Jules, *Crapshoot: Rolling the Dice on the Vice Presidency*, New York, Crown, 1992
Vice Presidents: A Biographical Dictionary, New York, Checkmark Books, 2001, L. Edward Purcell, editor,
    by L. Edward Purcell, pp 413-418
http://en.wikipedia.org/wiki/Dick_Cheney
http://www.washingtonmonthly.com/archives/individual/2004_06/004216.php
http://archives.cnn.com/2000/ALLPOLITICS/stories/07/24/bush.vp/index.html
http://www.thesmokinggun.com/archive/032206icheney1.html

Chapter 47: General Curtis LeMay
http://en.wikiquote.org/wiki/Curtis_LeMay
http://query.nytimes.com/gst/fullpage.html?res=990CEFD81F3AF931A25751C0A963958260
    &sec=&spon=&pagewanted=print
http://en.wikipedia.org/wiki/Curtis_LeMay
http://www.pbs.org/wgbh/amex/bomb/peopleevents/pandeAMEX61.html
http://faculty.smu.edu/dsimon/Change-Viet3b.html
http://www.time.com/time/magazine/article/0,9171,902372,00.html?promoid=googlep
http://www.time.com/time/magazine/article/0,9171,902426,00.html
http://www.time.com/time/magazine/0,9263,7601681018,00.html
http://www.washingtontimes.com/books/20070210-101939-4615r.htm
Witcover, Jules, *Crapshoot: Rolling the Dice on the Vice Presidency*, New York, Crown, 1992
http://en.wikipedia.org/wiki/George_Wallace#American_Independent_Party_presidential_
    candidate

http://en.wikipedia.org/wiki/Bikini_atoll
http://findarticles.com/p/articles/mi_m1316/is_n10_v27/ai_17612759/pg_2

Chapter 48: Thomas Eagleton
http://en.wikipedia.org/wiki/George_McGovern#1972_Presidential_election
http://www.time.com/time/magazine/article/0,9171,879139,00.html
http://www.answers.com/topic/thomas-eagleton
http://www.time.com/time/magazine/article/0,9171,906135-8,00.html
http://en.wikipedia.org/wiki/Image:ElectoralCollege1972-Large.png

Chapter 49: Representative Geraldine Ferraro
http://en.wikipedia.org/wiki/Geraldine_Ferraro

http://books.google.com/books?id=CNeStaJsKk8C&pg=PA99&lpg=PA99&dq=a+million+d
    ollar+rhymes+with+rich+barbara+bush+ferraro&source=web&ots=uonzOp84nf&sig=
    EuGg1mEICHMk1x2ᵈLdZjmeeYb7w&hl=en
http://eightiesclub.tripod.com/id330.htm
http://www.huffingtonpost.com/2008/03/10/clinton-backer-ferraro-0_n_90806.html
http://www.salon.com/opinion/conason/2008/03/14/ferraro_clinton/

Chapter 50: Admiral James Stockdale
http://en.wikipedia.org/wiki/1992_Demwwwocratic_presidential_primary
http://www.pbs.org/newshour/debatingourdestiny/92ᵈebates/vp1.html

Index

cherries,
    delicious with cold milk 68
    possibly poisoned with arsenic 68
Clinton, George 27, 28, 32, 36, 264
    befuddled 29
    drooling 28
    Mothership Connection Concert 312
coitus
    fatal 217
    interracial 52
    botched cover-up of fatal 217
    serial interracial 52
Colfax, Schuyler 87, 89, 92, 130, 268
companions, constant
    special secret 71
Coolidge, Calvin 145
Curtis, Charles 157

D

Dallas, George Mifflin 6, 61
Dawes, Charles Gates 151
death, agonizing 94
demon rum 37, 84.
Depression, Great
    casual dismissal of rampant horrors of 161
    inability to end 161

E

Eagleton, Thomas 255

F

face, shot in 249
Fairbanks, Charles 129
Ferraro, Geraldine 258
Fillmore, Millard 65, 66, 67, 68, 266
Ford, Gerald R. 209-211, 213, 215, 246, 250, 276
Franklin, Benjamin
    disparaging that buffoon Adams 13
    not touching the office with a ten-foot pole 6

G

H

I

J

K

L

M

S

T

U

V

W